Supporting the prime and specific areas of development

What does it mean to be three?

What every practitioner needs to understand about the development of three-year-olds

Jennie Lindon

Updated in accordance with the 2012 Early Years Foundation Stage

Contents

Published by Practical Pre-School Books, A Division of MA Education Ltd,
St Jude's Church, Dulwich Road, Herne Hill, London, SE24 0PB.
Tel: 020 7738 5454
www.practicalpreschoolbooks.com

ISBN 978-1-907241-40-6

Focus on three-year-olds

What does it mean to be three? covers the time span from when children are rising threes until they reach their fourth birthday. Significant developmental changes happen over these months, affecting young children and their families. Some boys and girls have already experienced time away from their parents. However, for other children, this is the year when they will join some kind of early years provision for part or all of their week. They may join a nursery or pre-school, they may spend time with a childminder – some threes will experience a combination of different types of provision.

The approach and ideas of this book are relevant to practitioners who are working with three-year-olds anywhere in the UK. However, the structure of the book follows the statutory framework for England of the Birth to Five Early Years Foundation Stage (EYFS). This new edition of *What does it mean to be three?* has been updated following the revised framework, implemented from September 2012. The main EYFS documents can be accessed through the Department for Education website (details on page 54). At the time of writing, Scotland is the only other nation in the UK that has specific guidance about best practice with under-threes (Learning and Teaching Scotland, 2010).

A learning journey across early childhood

In England, early years practitioners have been working within the EYFS since September 2008. The revised statutory framework and supporting guidance are much reduced in length and some details, like the early learning goals (ELGs) for the end of the stage, have been changed. Of course, everyone has to become familiar with the revised framework. Yet, early years provision with established best practice will not need to make sweeping changes to their approach to children and families. The crucial elements of best practice have not changed.

One focus of change is that the six areas of learning from the first EYFS framework have become seven areas, divided into three **prime** and four **specific** areas. This framework is one way of considering the breadth of children's learning. But of course babies and children do not learn in separate compartments; the whole point is that their learning crosses all the boundaries. The overall aim of identifying particular areas of learning is still to ensure that early years practitioners do not overlook important areas of development.

The rational for identifying the three prime areas of learning is that secure early development rests upon:

- Communication and language
- Physical development
- Personal, social and emotional development.

These three areas are identified as, '*particularly crucial for igniting children's curiosity and enthusiasm for learning, and for building their capacity to learn, form relationships and thrive*' (page 4, DfE 2012). The order above is the one given in the EYFS framework. I have moved personal, social and emotional development (PSED) to the front of the list for all the books in the *What does it mean to be…?* series. In terms of child development, it makes more sense to start with the crucial underpinning of PSED.

There is a sound developmental basis for arguing that, without secure personal, social and emotional development, toddlers and young children spend considerable energy striving for affirmation that they are accepted and loved for themselves. Concern has grown over the shaky communication skills of some young children, whose early experiences have not supported their development. Children's ability and motivation to be an active communicator – right from their earliest weeks and months – opens the door for other aspects of their development.

Making physical development a prime area is also welcome, since this aspect of how babies and young children learn has often been undervalued. Babies need safe space for movement and toddlers need to have easy opportunities to be physically active; encouraged by adult play partners who do not try to curb natural exuberance. There is good reason to be concerned about the well-being of young children whose limited opportunities for active play have already pushed them into sedentary habits.

The four specific areas are:

- Literacy
- Mathematics
- Understanding the world
- Expressive arts and design.

The guidance for early years practice is that the three prime areas should be uppermost in the minds of practitioners working with younger children. The age range has not been made specific, although the implication is that this different balance applies to working with under-threes. The four specific areas are still of relevance for very young children, but need to be fully understood in their baby, toddler or two-year-old version. Three-year-old learning, in these specific areas, evolves from developmentally appropriate experiences from their earlier years.

Over the year that children are three, your attention will be increasingly spread more evenly over the seven areas. You remain very alert to the prime areas, as the foundation for secure learning within the four specific areas. If over-threes are struggling within one or more of the prime areas of development, then your main focus must be there. You need to identify the nature of the problem and how you can best help children, in partnership with their family.

Early Education (2012) was commissioned by the DfE to produce the supporting non-statutory guidance across the Birth to Five age range. This document explains the four main themes of the EYFS: A Unique Child, Positive Relationships, Enabling Environments and how they contribute to the fourth theme, Learning and Development. The guidance also includes a revised version of 'Development Matters', cut back in line with the much reduced number of early learning goals (ELGs) for the end of the EYFS. This material offers ideas about how supportive practitioners behave with babies and children and what they could provide within the learning environment. These suggestions should refresh and inform best early years practice. They are not a have-to-do checklist.

The document provides some developmental highlights for a child's journey towards the early learning goals. This resource

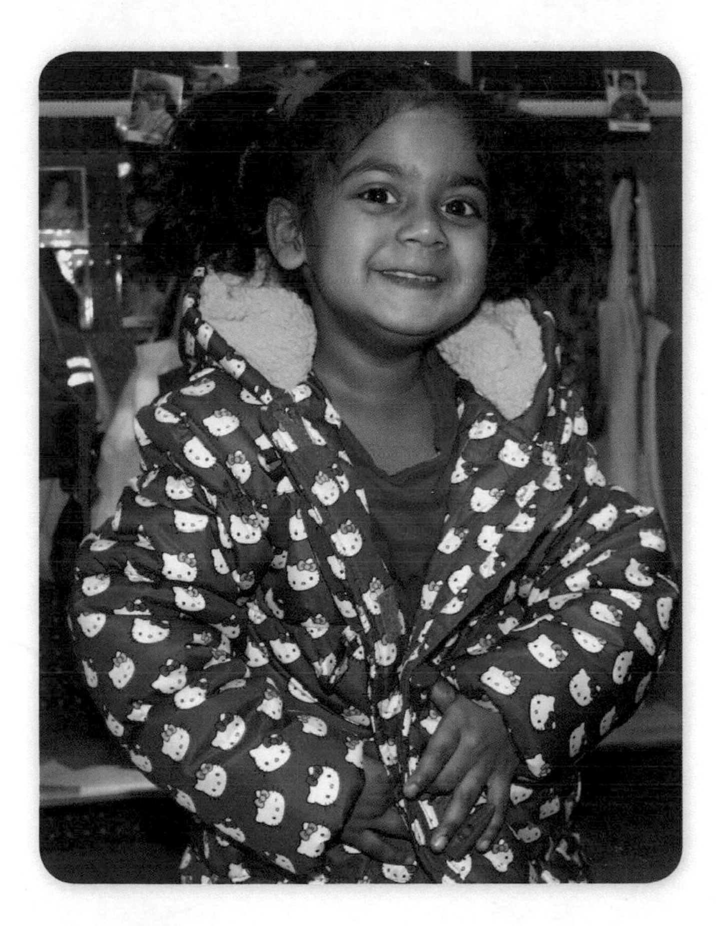

continues with the previous EYFS approach of broad and overlapping age spans: birth-to-11 months, 8-20 months, 16-26 months, 22-36 months, 30-50 months and 40-60+ months. The developmental information is a reminder of the kinds of changes likely to happen, if all is going well with babies and young children. They are, for instance, a brief reminder of the early part of the learning journey towards literacy or numeracy. The items are not an exhaustive list of everything that happens.

As with the first EYFS framework, these developmental highlights and linked practical advice, were neither developed, nor intended to be used, as a checklist to assess children. Their value is dependent on the secure child development knowledge of practitioners using the resource. The aim is to refresh realistic expectations, supporting practitioners to focus on the uniqueness of individual babies and children and to protect time for them to enjoy secure learning over early childhood. There should be no headlong rush to get threes into the 'older' age spans, let alone the final ELGs. Managers and practitioners all need to understand that none of the descriptions, with the sole exception of the ELGs, are required targets to be observed or assessed.

Child-focused observation and assessment

The revised EYFS continues to highlight the importance of ongoing observation, which enables practitioners to shape

learning experiences that are well-attuned to the interests and abilities of individual babies and toddlers. The revised statutory framework stresses that much of this observation arises within day-by-day alert looking and listening. Some practitioners call this informal or incidental observation and sometimes, not always, it may be captured with a brief written note or a photo.

All children should have a reliable and descriptive personal record, which will include some more organised observations. The revised EYFS gives very clear direction that the process of observation and assessment '*should not entail prolonged breaks from interaction with children, nor require excessive paperwork. Paperwork should be limited to that which is absolutely necessary to promote children's successful learning and development*' (page 10, DfE 2012).

The situation continues to be that, except for the EYFS profile, there are no statutory written formats for observation and assessment, nor for any kind of flexible forward planning. Early years settings and childminders can continue to use approaches that have worked well so far. The only difference is that layouts will need to be changed in line with the seven areas of development. Established best early years practice is not challenged by the revised EYFS framework.

Attentive and knowledgeable key persons will continue to be aware, and keep some records, of the progress of individual children over time. Observant practitioners will learn from watching, listening and being a play partner to children. These observations, often acted upon but not written down, will make a difference to the detail of what is offered to individuals and to sensible short-term changes in planned opportunities for a group of children. Flexible, forward planning will continue to be responsive to the needs and interests of individual babies and children: through continuous provision (the learning environment) and flexible use of planned activities.

The revised EYFS has introduced a new element to the statutory requirements for early years provision. From September 2012 there must be a descriptive individual assessment within the year that children are two: a two-year-old progress check; focused especially on the three prime areas of development. All early years provision with two-year-olds must organise this developmental assessment, by the key person. This check is described in detail in *What does it mean to be two?* (Practical Pre-School Books, 2012). For practitioners who work with three-year-olds, this progress check will be part of the existing record for individual children. When that assessment identified the need for additional help, then the key person will most likely still refer to the details. It will depend on how early within the year of being two that the progress check was completed.

The revised EYFS still applies to the end of the reception year, at which point children are assessed through a revised and much shorter EYFS Profile. The meaningless numerical scoring system has also disappeared. The total number of early learning goals (ELGs) has been significantly reduced from 69 to 17, and with some different wording. All the ELGs apply to the end of the phase of early childhood: specifically to the level of progress expected by the end of the summer term of the academic year in which a child reaches five years of age. It would make no developmental sense to attempt to apply any ELGs to three-year-olds.

Sound knowledge of child development

The effectiveness of any form of assessment, and the observations that support it, is highly dependent on the key person's child development knowledge. Practitioners must have realistic expectations for threes – whether young threes, in the middle of the year or rising fours. They are still very young children and in the normal course of events, a great deal happens over this twelve-month period.

Secure child development knowledge can be supplemented by the 'Development Matters' guidance materials mentioned on page 3. These developmental highlights are intended to remind and provoke further ideas about what you may have noticed. They are not a substitute for thorough knowledge of child development as a whole. This understanding must be covered within initial training for the early years workforce and then refreshed as part of continued professional development for everyone.

In terms of the overlapping age bands, practitioners working with younger threes will mainly look at the 30-50 months span. It makes good sense to look at the 22-36 months span, if you work with the just threes or children whose development has been significantly slowed by disability or very limited early experience. There should be no sense of rush, but it makes sense to begin with looking at the early parts of the 40-60+ months age band with older threes.

Depending on the form of provision, you may already have an established relationship with three-year-olds and their family, for whom you are the key person. On the other hand, you may have handled the children's transition into your group from a younger room, or as new arrivals to your whole provision. You may be getting to know these children as individuals, as well as applying your understanding of three-year-old development in general.

The family and yourself may already know that this child lives with a disability or a chronic health condition which significantly affects the pattern of development. However, it is possible that you will support threes, and their family, when it is not yet clear exactly what is affecting a delayed or unusual pattern of development. Usual good practice for partnership applies: you talk with parents to understand their child as an individual with familiar routines, likes and dislikes. Parents will be able to tell you, as a childminder or the child's key person in nursery, about their child's current ability level and any special help that will be needed.

You are not expected to know everything about every disability. Good practice is to know how to find out more. Parents will be experts about their own child but may not necessarily have had much help so far, especially if their young child's disability was not apparent until recently. In a group setting, the SENCO should have more specialised knowledge and local contacts.

The revised EYFS includes a strong theme of 'school readiness' (page 2, DfE 2012) and ensuring that children are 'ready for school' (page 4, DfE 2012). The well-being of young children rests on exactly how these phrases are interpreted in practice. The school years are important for children and they are the way that the majority experience their statutory education. However, early childhood should never be defined as the less important hallway leading into the big house that is school.

This issue is discussed in more detail in *What does it mean to be four?* (Practical Pre-School Books 2012). However, it needs a mention here, since a developmentally inappropriate interpretation of 'school readiness' results in the educational bullying of three year olds. Unrealistic demands for the end of the stage to deliver classroom-ready five-year-olds create a backwash that disrupts fours and, as a consequence, the learning journey for threes.

Healthy emotional development for young children is supported by a growing belief that they are competent individuals. They need a confident sense of 'I can' and that 'I can't yet' is not a disaster, because adults are supposed to help children who are struggling or have made a mistake. Best early years practice will enable young children to be ready for the version of reception class and then Year 1 that primary schools should offer. Responsible heads and their team should always focus on: 'Is our school ready for the children?' and not 'has somebody got them ready in ways that suit us?'.

Threes, and their younger selves, can develop that all important positive disposition to learn. They are curious, they want to find out more, use their skills and explore. In their own way, threes want to become more competent, to be able to express themselves, to climb that ladder and build that castle. Attentive and enthusiastic adults help children to develop this positive outlook over the months and years. They support even the most anxious girls or boys to keep trying, even if something is neither easy nor obvious at the outset. Familiar adults, led by the key person, foster a sense of personal satisfaction for individual children when they practise, improve and realise that they have managed a new skill or idea.

Personal, social and emotional development

Young girls and boys need to be respected for what they are at the moment. Their development unfolds in a secure way, because they are encouraged to relish what they are currently learning. Three-year-olds need to have had a well-supported year of being two and now they deserve the freedom to enjoy being three-year-olds.

Personal and emotional well-being

Young children attending any kind of early years provision need to be enabled to form close and affectionate relationships with familiar adults. Best early years practice has long integrated a 'key person approach', and this aspect continues to be statutory in the revised EYFS (Lindon, 2010). Rising threes and three-year-olds need to feel that they are noticed, liked and have become a valued part of any kind of group setting or their childminder's home. Those adults are responsive to the needs and individuality of young children. In a nutshell, adults need to care and show that they care about young children.

Some three-year-olds will be coping with separation from their parent(s) at this stage of their early experience. However, the separation experience will be different for individual children. Separating from the main carer will be a significant issue, when this setting is the first out-of home care for a child. But some three-year-olds continue in their nursery or with their childminder. Group early years provision usually has age-banded rooms, so the key person and parent may have worked closely together to ensure a happy transition from the room for under-threes. Of course, some threes have been waiting for the day they can join the nursery that has become familiar because of older siblings. The person most affected by the separation may be their parent, especially if this child is the youngest in the family.

Threes, just as much as younger children, need to feel emotionally safe and at ease with their important adults in their early provision. They need the reassurance that a cuddle and other forms of touch are available if they are sad, unwell or just a bit uncertain. However, affectionate touch is also part of friendly communication when young children, and you, are happy about something or so proud of what you have done together.

Three-year-olds are still very young children and it is important to emphasise this fact. They can be daunted and disheartened, if too much is expected of them and adults do not tune-in to the three-year-old outlook. On the other hand, with supportive adults and a friendly, accessible environment for learning, three-year-olds can be very competent in their chosen enterprises, articulate communicators and excellent company. Confidence is an invisible internal feeling but three-year-olds, like anyone else, show this feeling through their behaviour within a relaxed, well-resourced learning environment.

LOOKING CLOSELY AT THREES

In the garden of Mary Paterson Nursery School, the children were able to access a range of fixed and temporary climbing structures. I watched as over one day many threes and fours clambered over a structure made up of a sloping ladder connected to a pair of horizontal planks, supported by two bases, and a slide down the other side of the plank. Initially the planks were set close together and then, within the day, a practitioner pulled them slightly apart to create a further challenge.

LOOKING CLOSELY AT THREES

One aspect of experience, that becomes clear when you observe young children, is their delight in small spaces in their environment, as well as the larger spaces. In my time spent with Buckingham's Nursery, I could see the benefit for the children from adult thoughtfulness about creating 'cosy corners' in every room.

The senior team had worked with each room leader, so that every age group had an inviting indoor space where they could snuggle up. Each room had developed a slightly different space. The practitioners then watched to see how children used the resource over a couple of weeks and then adjusted accordingly.

Threes and fours were keen that I should see and get into their cosy corner, created by a lightweight tent, erected in one part of the room. Cushions and other items completed a very comfortable environment, used regularly by the children.

The layout gave children choice about how to deal with the balancing section. Some, like Josh (3yrs, 3mths) chose to manage the planks on their hands and knees. Josh came to the end and pushed the planks back together to ease his turn. Then he walked back upright until he reached the part where the two planks were creating a gap.

Josh levered himself between the planks to hang down and then dropped the short distance to the ground. He emerged, went to the slide end of the structure, climbed up to the planks. Then he said to me: "That's a trick. Shall I do it again?" I nodded and said an enthusiastic "yes". This time Josh put an arm over each plank and hung a few moments before dropping.

When you organise and manage time with children's well-being at the heart of your decisions, then you gain an understanding of what I call the 'big little things' that matter

PARTNERSHIP WITH PARENTS: UNFAMILIAR ROUTINES

Your own setting will seem familiar to you, but you will help three-year-olds and their parents or other family carers by looking at the environment and routines with a fresh eye.

For instance, what is the experience like for a three-year-old? What might be similar to home and what will be different? This question is not only for group settings; a childminder's home will have differences from this child's family home. You know your routines, but how do you, supported perhaps by your helpful four-year-olds, make these routines clear for newly arrived threes and their parents?

Most threes will already be familiar with routines: the pattern of their current day. So, if they look worried or seem uncooperative, you cannot conclude that a child is unable to understand or follow routines in general. They are most likely just puzzled by the unfamiliar way in which you run your day or session.

You may, of course, need to support threes from vulnerable families in which there has been little or no consistency for this child. Threes may also have been over-indulged within their family, with few or any boundaries set by their parents.

Then your task – and partnership with parents – will be different. You will be introducing the novel idea that there can be a reassuring predictability to the day, or that young children have to allow sometimes for the needs of other people.

in a child's world. By this phrase I mean that what may seem minor side issues to adults, can be a big new perspective for young children. The 'cosy corners' are one example of adults looking at what would add to a young child's sense of being 'at home' in their nursery.

Three year olds operate as individuals. They have a growing understanding of the world beyond their family and their nursery or childminder. These very young children learn by building on their own perspective and moving outwards to the slightly different lives of other people, still familiar to them. Their social world is grounded in what they know already and what makes sense to them from personal experience so far. Young children are sometimes described as 'egocentric'. This term is acceptable, so long as it is not weighted with the negative overtones of 'self-centred' or 'selfish'. Three-year-olds are focused on themselves and their own perspective. Their world definitely radiates out from 'me' and that is developmentally sound for their age.

Three-year-olds can be well able to attend, using their skills of looking and listening for what interests them, and often keen to involve familiar adults. Threes can be happy in small, intimate groups – no more than what I call a 'sofa-full'. They struggle to concentrate in larger groups, partly because threes find it hard to remain still, except for something that directly interests them. It is appropriate that you help threes to sit for a social lunchtime or for their self-service snack.

You do not want to squander their limited ability on adult-led, large group times.

Many three-year-olds relish a good conversation but they have difficulty with communication in big groups, including circle time. Rising threes and three-year-olds also find it very hard to wait in order to voice what they wish to say. From the three-year-old perspective, something interesting enough to share with adults or other children needs to be said right now or at the least very soon. Three-year-olds have always been like this. Unnecessary problems are created for them when practitioners are encouraged to import the developmentally inappropriate school classroom model into early years practice.

Social threes

Friends are important to threes and you will notice that some young boys and girls have already had the opportunity to establish close relationships. These friendships are sometimes between the same sex, but can definitely be between girls and boys. Some close companions are age

LOOKING CLOSELY AT THREES

Threes can be adept at one-off temporary social alliances in drop-in settings. However, genuine friendship can only develop when children meet each other on a regular basis, although not necessarily every day. Rising threes and 3-yr-olds can cope with a predictable pattern that they check with their parent or their key person.

At nearly three years of age, my daughter Tanith knew that Wednesday was the day she visited a drop-in at the nearby community nursery, accompanied by me or her nanny. Tanith had met and got on well with Matthew, who also attended each Wednesday. They both looked forward to meeting once a week in this predictable way. Tanith talked about meeting Matthew as we walked to the nursery and they had favourite corners in the nursery where they played.

Marie (3 years) was with a childminder each day and was the only child who attended every day of the week. However, as Marie's mother described to me, her daughter was completely clear about the pattern of attendance of the other children. Marie liked to check each morning what day of the week it was. She then had clear recall of which child(ren) she would see and play with today. Marie was confident about what would happen each day, and did not mind that she was the only full-week child. This pattern was normal for her.

LOOKING CLOSELY AT THREES

In New River Green I was at the dough table with four children, a mixed group of 3- and 4-yr-olds. I did not know any of the children's names and referred to one boy without being able to use his name. I asked Jake, 'Have you got some play dough for him?'.

Jake showed his 3-yr-old skills and told me the boy's name. It was an unusual name to me and I got it wrong, when I repeated it back to Jake. He was very patient and repeated the name twice, so I could say it correctly. Later in the day in another area of the nursery, Jake spontaneously told me the names of some other children. The likely explanation seemed to be that Jake wanted me to be able to address other children personally and properly. He understood the importance of names and was helping me to behave in a more social way.

peers. However, in my visits to nurseries, I noticed friendships (confirmed by practitioners) that had formed between a communicative, confident three-year-old and one or more four-year-olds.

Young girls and boys cannot establish friendships, if their potential friends are attending on completely different patterns. In recent years the watchword from government initiatives (Labour and the Coalition government) has been 'flexible' patterns of attendance. It is noteworthy that this concept is applied to early years provision, but never to the school years. Children from an emotionally secure family background want to have a predictable pattern to their days and weeks. The usual needs of young children are heightened for young boys and girls from vulnerable families, who may already be dealing with a topsy-turvy world. These children desperately need more and not less predictability. Highly flexible patterns of attendance are unlikely to offer positive experiences for three-year-olds or any under-fives.

It would be appropriate to be concerned about children who show a serious lack of social skills; with difficulty in relating to other children even when they have had time to settle and you observe them in quiet, apparently relaxed situations. Some children, who are later found to have some level of autistic spectrum disorder, are noticed as three-year-olds whose development already contrasts with their peers. Children may show confusion in relations with other children, are anxious about the most minor changes of routine and perplexed by the kind of play, especially pretend play, that most three-year-olds can manage.

Three-year-olds do not only make close social contact with their age peers or slightly older children. Threes often like contact with younger children, including toddlers and babies, when that opportunity is available to them. In full age-range nurseries and childminders' homes, there are social gains for everyone in contact across the ages of early childhood. Contact between the ages is part of normal family life and of friendship between local families. I have visited many nurseries who ensure that older children can have regular contact with the younger ones, and not only siblings – as important as that contact is for children who are in different base rooms.

Three-year-olds can be adept at the repetitive games that babies and toddlers adore and at making them chortle. These still young children often like to 'read' to toddlers by telling a story to the pages and illustrations of a very familiar book. You will sometimes observe that threes, especially the older threes, adjust their style of communication for babies and toddlers. They show an understanding – a level of empathy – that babies and toddlers need simpler words and more gestures. Alert threes may be copying the adjusted speech and body language of a familiar adult. Yet, this alert imitation still shows an impressive level of understanding.

Best early years practice is to organise a flexible day and a welcoming learning environment. Young children can then easily make choices about with whom they will play, their seating companions at the lunch table or when and with whom they will have their drink and fruit within a self-service snack time. Young boys and girls cannot make relaxed social contact with each other, if adults – practitioners or parents – keep organising and re-organising the children.

LOOKING CLOSELY AT THREES

In Mary Paterson Rumpus Drop-in, Rebecca (3yrs, 3mths) was involved with the wooden train track and trains for a sustained period of time (see also pages 17 and 23). For most of her play, Rebecca was able to organise this resource to her own satisfaction. However, at one point, the railway track she had built single-handedly had to be shared.

Steven (19 months) had placed his train on the final section and was pulling it along towards Rebecca's train. The possible crash was resolved because Rebecca took her train back over the bridge and onto the loop. Then she faced an impossible turn. Yet, Rebecca persevered to leave Steven his bit of track. She used a solution she had devised earlier and remade the train on the lower side of the loop. Rebecca was very careful getting the wheels back onto the wooden track – the carriages and trucks joined magnetically.

Soon Rebecca's train was right by Steven's train. He made protesting noises and his mother helped initially by making a gap between the trains. However, Rebecca resolved the impasse by saying: "You go first". The two children now moved their trains at the same time. Steven ran his train off the end of the track and moved away.

You help by having a predictable pattern to the day or session, which has plenty of scope for threes to organise themselves. Of course, you are easily available – as a considerate play partner, to join in conversation and to be the diplomat when those skills are needed. Your contribution is to be generous with your time and attention for individual children and intimate groups. Three-year-olds who have to compete for adult attention or affection have limited emotional energy to make social contact with their 'rivals'.

Threes continue to enjoy playing sometimes on their own, or with an adult rather than a child companion. Adults are often concerned about children who seem to be isolated, or who are apparently rejected in play by their peers. However, for children themselves, the problem may be more about how to deal with a child who wants to play with them, but the first child does not want their play interrupted. It is often not appropriate to insist that the busy child should let the second child play too. The adult task is often to enable both children to play with a resource that can accommodate more than one child. Yet, sometimes you will observe that even young threes have the skills, and the motivation, to resolve some play issues without your direct help.

Feeling and behaving

Rising threes and three-year-olds experience a wide range of feelings. However, they are towards the beginning of their learning journey of ways to express those emotions through actions and words. They still have much to learn about the feelings of other people; children, but also the surprising revelation that adults have feelings too.

Rising threes and three-year-olds will not always have the words to name what they feel. Much depends on how far their familiar adults have set a good example of using an emotional vocabulary. When threes spontaneously announce: "I'm cross about…" or "I think she's very sad…", you are seeing the evidence of past experience. Familiar adults – parents and practitioners – have responded naturally to situations that arose. Adults have used the words for feelings appropriately in context, with a full understanding of three-year-old development. You cannot teach children about feelings or promote emotional literacy through adult-planned activities. Threes and then fours learn from real events and the reactions of emotionally literate adults.

Threes, especially the younger ones, can move at speed from happiness and excitement to distress or frustration. Their normal state is to be very focused in the moment and their loss of a favourite bike can be a crisis. Over a long day, threes also get tired. In a nurturing environment, practitioners recognise that this child's tipping point is swifter when they need a quiet time, if not an actual nap. It is a serious challenge for threes to re-direct themselves once their emotions have welled and very strong feelings sometimes frighten them. They need to feel emotionally safe in order to calm down. Such support often needs to be physical: the comfort of touch and cuddle and sometimes the safety of your arms that communicate non-verbally, 'I'm not going to let you hurt yourself or anyone else'.

Three-year-olds are also learning what to do, and the consideration to expect for yourself, when social communication goes awry. Adults are sometimes very insistent that children say 'sorry'. Yet an inflexible approach is more likely to convince children that this particular 'magic word' stops people nagging you. Three-year-olds often cannot predict the consequences of their actions and sometimes there has been a genuine accident. Given time and choices, three-year-olds become more able and willing to show 'sorry' by making amends. With adult support, threes steadily learn more about the feelings of the child, or adult, who has been bumped or left out of play. Older threes even may even begin to grasp the concept of the emotional consequences for other people – the idea of 'hurting inside'.

Three-year-olds do not learn to be 'considerate' or 'kind' in one big developmental step, nor do they show this kind of behaviour every minute of every day. Threes, who feel emotionally secure with you, are happy sometimes to help another child, take turns even on a prized item of equipment and to offer comfort in times of distress. They will not be able to explain why these actions are the 'right' way to behave – and this does not matter at all. Older threes are probably close to the valuable perspective that it is 'much nicer if we are friendly to each other' or the warm feel of 'I help and she helps me'.

Three-year-olds often want to please adults who are kind themselves, but young girls and boys have only a hazy idea of the underlying principles and reasons. They need simple explanations linked to experiences that make sense to them. Threes can take on board simple ground rules that make sense in their familiar environment – family as well as early years provision. Three-year-olds struggle with abstract rights and wrongs, but they are keen observers of what people do and say. If adults fail to set a good example about the behaviour they want, then children are likely to follow adults' actions rather than fine words. Some threes, especially those who listen to older children, are also likely to embrace their first philosophical concept – that of fairness – although they will probably get 'that's so unfair' before 'that's the fair thing to do'.

Three-year-olds have developed skills of attention; of looking and listening. Given an activity of interest to them and avoidance of interruption, many threes can concentrate very well and are increasingly able to get themselves back to the activity if the diversion is mild or of their own choosing. Threes find it difficult to concentrate when they are required to keep still and quiet for no good reason that they can decipher. They do not benefit from large group sit-down times. In contrast, threes can be absorbed and very chatty in small, intimate groups.

PARTNERSHIP WITH PARENTS: ACCEPTANCE OF FEELINGS

The feelings expressed, or suppressed, by three-year-olds, will reflect their experiences so far in their family but also in any early years provision prior to joining you.

You will observe some threes who confidently use a range of words for feelings, as well as the phrases that communicate fellow feeling, like 'you alright?' However, the key person will need to look for opportunities to share a different perspective with parents, or grandparents, who prefer not take children's feelings seriously or do not want to observe certain emotions. Children may have been told "there's nothing to be frightened about; it's only a worm" or "take that look off your face!".

Even threes are learning about feelings that are acceptable to adults and those which are better hidden. Perhaps, they are not supposed to get 'over excited' or now believe that 'big boys don't cry'.

Child-friendly routines

Three-year-olds are on the road towards independence, but this is a steady process. With time and discreet adult support, young children are becoming self-reliant within daily routines and are already able to share in much of their own care.

Three-year-olds can usually manage much of their own toileting and simple hygiene like hand washing. They should be able to feed themselves and handle drinks, although not all the time and there will be some spillage. So long as adults have not done everything for them so far, threes will manage a great deal of their dressing and undressing. They will need help for the trickier fastenings and elements; shoelaces (if they have them) are difficult for some time yet.

Three-year-olds who are confident in your provision will manage a great deal on their own in terms of making choices and handling daily routines. Children experience personal satisfaction when they have a genuine part to play in domestic routines; they can be genuinely helpful within this familiar context. Young children are far happier to get busy with the tidying or to be trusted to lay the table than to sit around waiting, while an adult does this domestic task 'because it's quicker'.

Threes also learn a considerable amount through this involvement. Some very practical early mathematical experiences arise through welcoming children as active working members of your nursery or home. They relish involvement in simple 'administration' such as running simple messages or returning the register to the office in a nursery. Three-year-olds learn a great deal through play, but they certainly do not only learn through what adults would classify as play.

LOOKING CLOSELY AT THREES

Threes can show impressive confidence in a familiar environment, including putting a visitor at ease, as I experienced in New River Green. I sat with Rosie (3 years) in an area equipped with a table and pull-out drawers with jigsaws as well as other materials.

Rosie started to chat, telling me her plans: "I'm going to do drawing (pause) I'm going to do the puzzle, then drawing and then I'm going to go outside". She was able to pull out the drawer and choose a wooden jigsaw. We tipped it out onto the table. Rosie used her finger to hop from piece to piece and she sang a tuneful ditty that was mainly the words "Froggy, froggy, froggy".

Rosie told me, "I can't do this puzzle" but it soon became clear that she knew very well how to sort out the pieces and fit them together. I said "you were teasing me. You can do this puzzle". Rosie giggled in reply. In between completing the puzzle with confidence, Rosie commented and showed me other items of interest close by. She focused back onto the puzzle each time with no difficulty.

LOOKING CLOSELY AT THREES

In Mary Paterson Nursery School, lunchtime is a valued part of the day. There was plenty of time for a good meal and conversation too. The children were fully active in this routine, for their own meal and as individual helpers each day, who lay the tables.

The children served themselves as much as possible. The food was in containers that children could pass between each other. The adult on each table eased the process with comments like "well done", "pass it on to Kerry", "you can put the spoon in and then pass it on to Mohammed". The children poured drinks for themselves from jugs on the table and often went to refill a jug from the water filter in the corner of the room. They also offered to pour for their peers, without any prompting from an adult. I watched several examples of one child asking another: "Do you want some water?".

The practitioner at each table, including the head, always eats with the children. This best practice brings alive the healthy eating message through adult behaviour. Practitioners also gave friendly guidance about mealtime etiquette, for instance the reminder that: "If you've touched the bit of bread, it's yours". The adults took natural opportunities to name individual foods: "I'm going to have some of the jambalaya" and "I'm going to have some peas – they're my favourite".

Children tidied up their own plates into the special lunchtime arrangement on the wooden cover over the large water equipment stand. They had learned the system of using a black bin bag for leftover food, a bowl for cutlery and the flat surface to pile the plates. Child helpers also emptied the large vegetable dishes into the bin and slotted the dish back into the larger containers for removal later. The children also understood to put the metal lids on the dishes once they are back in the containers. At the end of their meal, the children wiped their personalised table mat and put it away, along with their apron.

Communication and language

Three-year-olds can be effective communicators, using their own spoken language as well as awareness of the body language of familiar adults and children. The skills of young boys and girls develop through relaxed communication and spontaneous conversation, which is an integral part of the day. Three-year-olds, like any young children, do not need structured language programmes unless something has gone awry with the usual pattern of development.

Chatty threes

Rising threes and three-year-olds are a varied group, depending on their temperament as well as their experiences to date. Some are far more chatty, articulate and questioning than their fellow three-year-olds. However, even the young threes should have a large enough vocabulary that it is a challenging task to note down all their words and the ways in which they spontaneously them.

If everything has progressed normally and well, then three-year-olds do not simply have a large vocabulary; they know and use different types of words. Children who are known to have a disability affecting language or a specific language disorder will need specially focused help. However, some threes are not talking much because familiar adults have not bothered to talk much with them – in family life, or if children have experienced poor quality early years provision.

If you work with threes whose early experiences have done them no favours, it is important to recall how toddlers and twos build their vocabulary, when all is well. Whereabouts are these vulnerable threes in their language development? A toddler's first set of words are the names of familiar people and objects that they see and handle in daily life. In terms of grammar, these words are the nouns. If language development is progressing without difficulties, then older toddlers, and certainly young twos, are also using a range of words that apply to actions (the verbs). These words describe what people are doing or what the child wants to have happen. Does this delayed three-year-old use action as well as naming words?

Once a young child has naming and action words, then they have the conceptual and language base to use words that communicate very simple ideas. With ordinary encouragement in personal interaction, twos show that they are ready to describe characteristics of the world around them – meaningful to this individual child. They use words that add to the naming words or the action words. A two-word comment like 'noisy dog' is an example of an adjective added to a noun, and will often be accompanied by a pointing finger, to ensure you look at what has caught this child's attention. A request for 'run fast' – a lively dash about the garden – is an example of adding an adverb to provide additional description to the verb. Does this child use descriptive words?

Best early years practice will always be to help children on from their current position. If your provision has a high proportion of threes, whose language development has been delayed, part of your professional responsibility is to keep a firm hold on usual progress for this age group. Twos should be talking; there is a significant problem when threes are not talking. However, If you lose track of normal development, then ordinarily chatty threes or very young fours appear to be outstanding.

Three-year-olds who experience a relaxed and communicative atmosphere will continue to add new words, as well as combine their words in phrases that show their ability to use language to different purposes. Threes, especially the slightly older threes, are able to ask you the meaning of an unfamiliar word. Three-year-olds, who have had varied experiences, develop their own interests that are reflected in a slightly more specialist vocabulary. Their spontaneous conversation, and wish to inform you, will show their enthusiasm for lorries and big buses, dinosaurs, fantasy or real creatures and what spiders get up to in their webs.

Young children sometimes become sticklers for accuracy about items within a broadly similar group, for example;

LOOKING CLOSELY AT THREES

It is important that adults follow the flow of what children want to talk about, although sometimes you will start chatting. In a friendly, conversational atmosphere, young children do not have to be persuaded to talk. These examples are from New River Green.

Lynne (a practitioner) had arrived at the table with a fresh batch of bright red play dough. She ladled out some of it on the table, explaining that the rest was for the toddlers. Lynne also explained that the dough was still hot. Rosie (3 years) and Tyrone (4 years) were very interested in the dough. Rosie wanted to know why the dough was hot and Lynne explained that she had just cooked it fresh for everyone. Tyrone wanted to know how Lynne had cooked the dough. Both children were fascinated with the fact that the dough was not yet cool and they tentatively touched it. The dough was now warm rather than hot.

In New River Green, Rosie recalled in the afternoon the time she and I had spent together in the morning (page 12). We walked together in the garden and Rosie commented: "You went away when I had my milk". I replied: "You were busy, so I went to another part of the nursery". Rosie then continued: "I didn't do another jigsaw because you'd gone". I answered: "I'm sorry I'd gone. But I did enjoy doing the jigsaw and looking at the fish with you".

Winston (3 years) and Jon (3 years) in New River Green found and put on hard hats, one yellow and one red. Winston said: "I'm Bob the Builder" and the practitioner nearby replied, "hello Bob". Jon indicated Winston and says "two Bob the Builders". Rosie who was at a nearby table, pointed to the hard hat and said "that's a real one". A conversation followed about Jon's brother who had a woolly 'Bob the Builder' hat for the winter. The two boys continued building their constructions with the blocks, singing the 'Bob the Builder' song.

LOOKING CLOSELY AT THREES

In Poplar Play, Charlotte (3 years) and Alric (3 years) were playing with wooden trains and small blocks. I was sitting close by and Charlotte started to chat with me. I expressed genuine interest and listened, but Charlotte definitely led this conversation.

Charlotte started with "these are my new socks" and pulled up her trouser legs to show me properly. She explained: "I bought them in John Lewis with my Mum", then "we bought five socks". Counting partly on her fingers, Charlotte recalled three of the five types of sock they had bought. She then announced "and we bought tights for Mum". Charlotte continued with... "I have new slippers. They have special lights on" and she indicated where by running her finger round the edge of her shoes.

I made a comment that "there aren't any lights on your shoes" and Charlotte corrected me "they are trainers". She was right and Alric, who had been listening, showed me his footwear, explaining: "These are trainers too". We had a short chat about what made them trainers and the children pointed out the key features.

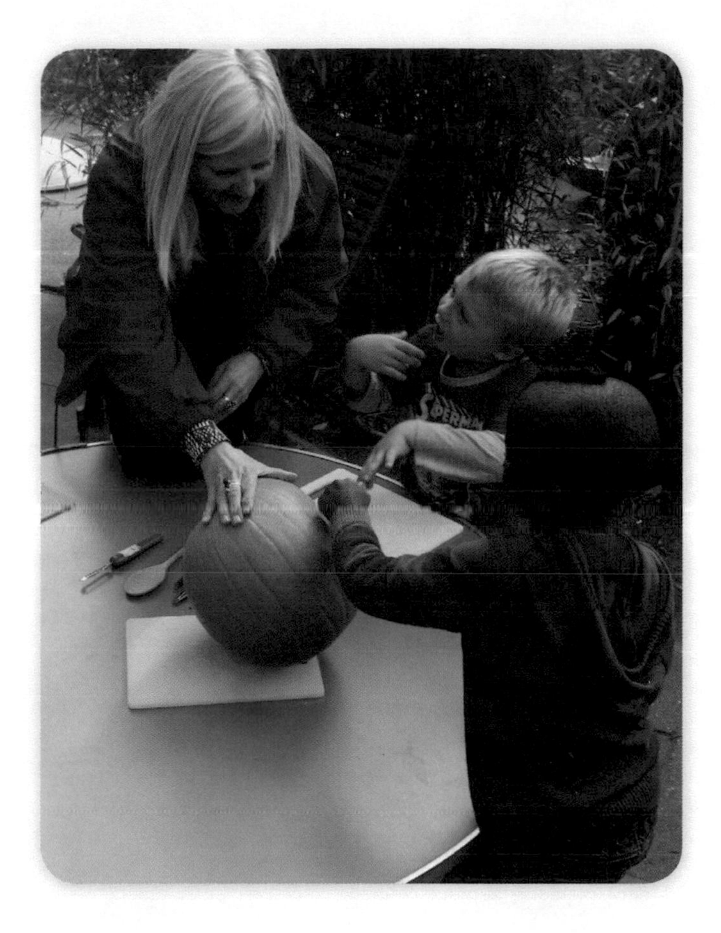

what is a cup and what is a mug? I noted how my own son, Drew, over the year that he was three, wanted to know the difference between a wood and a forest, then between a tunnel and a bridge – since these two were sometimes combined in the same structure. Sometimes it matters a great deal to young children that they sort out the distinctions within a category of items.

The Poplar Play conversation (example on this page) remained low key and low volume. However, I have been part of conversations in which children have become intense over key definitions. I recall acting as the diplomat in a heated exchange in a nursery garden between two older threes and a four-year-old over what exactly was the difference between a sandal and a shoe. The volume rose and was accompanied by firm sticking out of feet to demonstrate that this was definitely a sandal and that, pointing, was not.

Three-year-olds are much clearer now about how objects relate together in ways that they can see and directly experience. So they are more likely to use words like 'in', 'on' or 'under' that describe simple connections between objects – grammatically, the prepositions. Three-year-olds use a very wide variety of grammatical structures and they learn both the regular and irregular grammatical forms by listening to what is said in their hearing. English is an especially difficult language with exceptions to practically every grammatical rule, as well as very complex spelling. So it is usual that three-year-olds – and fours or fives too – make mistakes by extending the basic rule to words that are exceptions. An example is saying 'eated' rather than 'ate', since the normal rule from present to past tense is to add '-ed', as in 'I walked to nursery today'.

Of course three-year-olds and their slightly older companions learn the grammatical forms that they hear from adults and children in their neighbourhood. Different versions of English, between social and cultural groups, often use variations in the basic grammar: for instance 'we was..' rather than 'we were..', or 'me' instead of 'I'. Later on, in primary school, children will learn the differences between spoken and written forms of the language.

You should be able to observe three-year-olds using their language to serve different ends in their play, conversation with children and adults and their involvement in daily routines. The examples throughout this section show threes' ability to narrate what they are doing and direct their own play. These young boys and girls can use their language to tell and describe as a part of a conversation. They are able to share immediate interests, but also to recall incidents in the past and to plan a little into the future. In a simple version, three-year-olds can explain, justify and sometimes argue their point of view. The fact that sometimes they may be arguing with us, the adults, should not mean we overlook their impressive use of language.

Rising threes and three-year-olds need personal conversation. They may manage an active group time

with songs and stories, especially with an adept adult storyteller and props. However, they are too young for pre-planned exploration of ideas and issues in large group activities like circle time. A spontaneous conversation that develops around the lunch or dough table is a far more valuable opportunity. Three-year-olds need plenty of scope to explore their own perspective and experience. Adult planning and informal small group experiences are important. Your thoughtfulness and looking ahead is best used to ensure local outings like the example on this page.

LOOKING CLOSELY AT THREES

A small group from Mary Paterson Nursery School took a local walk lasting about an hour and a quarter. The aim was to reach good viewpoints for two building sites but the different routes out and back to nursery were taken at a relaxed pace.

The head had told me how even the quieter children chose to chat on these regular local trips, and she was absolutely right. Children started chatting as soon as we were on the street. They wanted to know: "How will we get to the building?" and "do we need to go past my house?". There was the anticipation of "...and I'll show you my house". The group stopped to look at one child's home and took photos.

Opportunities were taken – as on all outings – to involve the children in active road safety drills. The route took in crossings with red and green figures, a zebra crossing and the need to find a safe place to cross when there were no official crossing points. Children were reminded, in a friendly way, to keep looking and listening even when they had 'green man' on their side.

The two building sites were different and it was also possible to take a peek at the site office. One building site could be seen through safety gates with glimpses of what was going on inside the partially completed building. The second site was more open. Standing across the road from the site, we had clear views of the cranes, men working with diggers and dump trucks and others directing the activity. Children's comments and questions flowed.

Children were interested in many different features of this circular walk. One child was keen to point out to me every instance of 'my bus', (the number 6), on which he travelled to nursery with his parent. Some beautiful hanging baskets were admired in one street.

Talking and thinking

Babies and toddlers show us that they are thinking and remembering, but they communicate through their actions. As their spoken language develops and extends, young children are able to tell us as well. They learn to use spoken words for thinking out loud and for self direction.

Threes like to talk about ideas or possibilities that make sense in their social world. However, three-year-olds need to speak their thoughts and to voice an idea out loud very soon after thinking it. This situation applies over early childhood; young girls and boys find it tough to keep quiet if something has interested or intrigued them. They want to share and that is the reason they need a conversational home or nursery and not a classroom setting, with its more formal group approach.

When three-year-olds say something out loud, the verbal action helps to firm up their thoughts and opinions. Their self-talk, a kind of private running commentary, gives their ideas and plans in play a more definite form. Young children benefit from being active in their language in order to support their thinking, and guide their actions in a more complicated sequence of pretend play or complicated construction enterprises. Three-year-olds literally think out loud and young children continue to do so until more like seven years of age.

Young children benefit from hearing familiar adults sometimes talk their thoughts out loud within shared activities – joint play or working together on domestic tasks within a relaxed routine to the day or session. Of course, wise adults do not talk non-stop, nor do you simply empty the contents of your mind at any given moment. You comment in a meaningful way about what you are doing, hitches or puzzles in your current plan or simply voice out loud the 'what next..?' in a joint enterprise with young children.

Whose questions?

Three-year-olds are usually able to adjust their language depending on the purpose of communication, activity, mood and the listener. They vary tone and emphasis to convey feelings like excitement. Three-year-olds are confident in the pattern of asking questions as well as replying to them. They use question words: 'what/where/when?' and sometimes more than one repeat of 'why?'. But they also convey questioning by the tone in their voice. Some three-year-olds pose questions that make you think about the answer or the best way to word your reply.

With normal progress, three-year-olds have gained the understanding that words represent real objects. For instance, two-year-olds who are asked, "what is a ball?" assume that the adult questioner is confused about what a ball looks like and will point to a picture, or they search for a ball to show and demonstrate. Three-year-olds increasingly understand that this kind of question, as worded, means 'tell me something about a ball' and will make comments like, 'it bounces' or 'I play tennis with my ball'. This change is a significant step for more abstract thought.

Three-year-olds are making the move into language as a tool and a means to handle abstract ideas. When three-year-olds are learning new concepts, they still need a concrete situation in which to ground the idea. But their questions show how, with more familiar ideas or close conceptual links, they can explore through language alone. These still very young children have made an exciting shift into 'what if…' This speculation about reality includes the words to launch into explorations, such as 'what if we pretend to be fireman and we put out a fire in the home corner'. The 'what if...' rich possibilities in child-initiated play are also fully supported by threes' use of their physical skills. This development struggles to unfold if early years practitioners lose their way and over-organise children's play.

Questions have a place in communication: from the child to you and from you to the children. But you do not want your use of questions to unbalance communication, nor for children to gain the impression that adults usually ask the questions and children give the answers. There are times when a closed question, requiring a simple or one-word answer, is appropriate. Examples would be: "Has anybody seen where I put my glasses?" or "would you like another baked potato?".

LOOKING CLOSELY AT THREES

In Mary Paterson Rumpus Drop-in, Rebecca (3yrs, 3mths) was involved with the wooden train track and trains for a sustained period of time.

As she built up her train plus carriages, Rebecca commented on what was happening: "They all go through the tunnel/they're so heavy/oh no/there we go". Rebecca faced the practical problem of getting her very long train over the bridge and onto a tight circle of track. She asked her mother: "How are we going to get to that bit?". Her mother suggested following the track, holding the train steady with her finger. With her mother's verbal encouragement, Rebecca was successful without direct help: "There we go" and "we're in the middle".

Rebecca used self talk as she guided her train, gesturing around the loop saying "same direction, same direction". Her mother gave her the word 'tilted' to describe the steep angle of the train as Rebecca guided it along and off the bridge section. She focused on taking her train around the loop again, going "chugga chugga" and re-using her solution for the tight turn to reach the bridge.

Rebecca continued with her play, saying: "Everyone, stay on the train carefully". She commented to her mother "it's really long". Rebecca counted the carriages up to five and then lost count. She was not yet finger counting.

PARTNERSHIP WITH PARENTS: 'SELF-TALK' IS POSITIVE

The importance of children's private, out loud speech may not be clear to parents. You may be able to reassure some fathers or mothers that guiding self-talk is not only perfectly normal in early childhood, but is also a positive development. The key person can explain, using examples from the parent or carer's child, the delight for you of hearing a child share their thinking out loud.

You can talk with parents, even those who are at ease with threes' self-talk, and share that this form of communication gradually becomes more of a quiet mutter and turns into inner speech: children's unspoken thoughts. Remind parents that adults often return to talking out loud, although relatively quietly, when we face something new, especially challenging or complex.

Practitioners or parents who require children to be quiet – perhaps as evidence that the child is concentrating – will actually block young thinking and learning.

A useful balance from adults needs a range of open-ended questions and questioning requests. These are adult comments to which there are several possible answers, for instance: "That's a very interesting fact about spiders. How did you discover that?", or "any ideas about how we can unravel all this string?". A helpful underlying approach from adults is to have a good proportion of 'I wonder' or 'How about...?' kind of questions.

It is best to avoid a focus on testing questions – where you already know the answer and your aim is to check if the child knows. This approach soon becomes cross-questioning to children, and significantly reduces your value as a conversational play partner. Be patient, watch and listen; you will very soon realise that individual children can distinguish these colours or count these objects. If you remain unsure, then threes will not mind guiding questions in a playful context, such as "let's see if we can find...?" or "who's got sharp eyes here?".

Adults – practitioners and parents – need to resist the temptation to ask lots of questions, as well as giving young children more information that they want today. With the best of intentions, we sometimes talk too much. Of course, young children are not well supported by familiar adults who say hardly anything at all in response to threes, or who fend off children's comments or questions with, 'not now'. However, a genuine conversation is a shared event, characterised by give-and-take, listening as well as talking and, from adults, willingness to embrace the child's purpose in striking up this exchange.

In genuine conversation, as in play, early years practitioners must not seize the children's moment for adult purposes.

LOOKING CLOSELY AT THREES

Emma was working with Karim (4yrs, 3mths) to prepare the raised bed for new plants and was joined after a short while by Qasim (3yrs, 7mths) and Lisa (3yrs, 2mths) joined the working group. Karim was busy raking and Emma explained how they needed to get all the twigs out. This was focused physical work and Karim commented that "this is hard". The adult suggested: "You can take your coat off if you're hot" and Karim did remove his coat.

Emma asked: "Are you ready to get your hands dirty? Can you reach that corner?". They were smoothing it down together. Emma explained they needed the surface smooth. She and the children were building up the bed with new earth, which they fetched from a store of fresh earth on the other side of the garden. Emma suggested: "Let's get one more bucket" and commented on "using your muscles". Qasim and Lisa went off holding a larger container – one to each handle to get more earth. They tried to lift the container full of earth but this was too heavy and they needed help.

Emma said to all of them; "Are you ready to get your hands dirty?" and helped Lisa to push up her sleeves. As they worked, a conversation unfolded from Emma's wondering question of "what helps plants grow?". Karim was clear that they need "water". When prompted by Emma: "Yes, what else?", Karim added "the sky" and reached "the sun".

Emma explained to Lisa about watching out for the few sweet pea plants that were still growing. She showed how take out twigs and dead leaves because "they're not growing anymore". Emma also explained that "this is new soil – we got it delivered. What do you think guys? Do you think we need one more bucket of soil? We need it up to the top". Karim and Lisa set off together for another bucket load and Emma followed to help.

LOOKING CLOSELY AT THREES

Mohammed, Harry and Jessica (a mix of threes and fours) spent twenty minutes in sustained pretend play with the table of animal figures. They had crocodiles, giraffes, tigers and hippos with small cut-offs of wood, bark, twigs, and leaves. Initially, the children had Gayatri (a practitioner) with them and then they were playing on their own.

All three children were especially interested in the fact that crocodiles behaved in a fierce way, that they ate people and crunched things. Harry put twigs in the crocodile's mouth and said "he's snapping the branch". Then in the middle of the conversation about creatures who ate people, Mohammed wanted to talk a bit about a recent event. He asked "where is that man?' and Gayatri explained that the person was a visitor to the nursery, so was not here today.

Jessica lined up a group of giraffes and counted them – correctly up to five: "I'm making a house for the giraffes". Harry was also keen to make a house for the animals. They had cylindrical wood cut-offs which they used to build a house together.

Gayatri commented that "sometimes crocodiles look like logs". The two boys were interested in this idea: that people might step on crocodiles by accident. Gayatri then added the idea that crocodiles may lay in a swamp waiting. Mohammed was making his crocodile eat everything and asked: "Do you think a crocodile could kill a tiger?". A short conversation followed around that theme, sometimes with the children making an animal figure eat another figure.

Physical development

The revised EYFS has placed physical development centre stage, as one of the three prime areas. This change is welcome, since it should challenge the tendency to undervalue children's physical development in favour of what seem, to some adults, to be the more important intellectual areas. Research into child development has to share some of this responsibility. Developmental psychology has tended to describe the changes in physical abilities, without much consideration of what they mean for children's learning as a whole. There has historically been considerably more interest in studying the development of communication and cognitive ability.

Physical confidence matters

Young children's physical development is important for their all-round development and well-being. When you watch toddlers turn into twos and twos into threes, you can see that young children's physical growth makes new behaviours possible. With their increased mobility and confidence, the accessible environment for young girls and boys gradually extends. Threes still want your help sometimes, but to their delight they can organise themselves much more.

As with all areas of learning, early years practitioners need to keep hold on realistic expectations. Some limits are perfectly normal, for instance, threes – especially the older threes – can be impressive climbers and bikers. However, they do not have the coordination to hit balls with bats in a planned way. You will not get a threes cricket team; it does not matter how hard you try. However, interested threes will get better at connecting a manageable bat to connect with a ball that is rolled along the ground at them. They cannot throw balls through basketball hoops, but they will make a good try at throwing a ball or a bean bag into a large container set on the ground.

Now that children are three, you will see the consequences of their earlier experiences – at home or in early years provision. Have younger children had time, space and adult encouragement to use their skills, getting better all the time – like the two-year-olds in this example? Or do you now observe threes who have been restricted by adults who dominated the play and over-protected by edgy practitioners or parents?

If all goes normal and well, young children's increased physical confidence supports their independence, a self-reliance appropriate for their age. Three-year-olds who can fasten and unfasten their own coat and shoes have more

direct control about moving on to the next part of their day. They do not have to wait for adult help, although in the settings mentioned in this book, the children looked confident that help was there should they need it.

Three-year-old play companions show their personal satisfaction when they can move around play resources like loads of cardboard boxes and other recycled materials, to announce later: "We did this all on our own!". The physical skills that support co-operative play also provide the context for social interaction and rich communication. Children enjoy organising and building together, planning and making something happen.

The importance of movement

Three-year-olds need plenty of opportunities for vigorous play, within a learning environment that is well-resourced – indoors and especially outdoors. Best early years practice never lost respect for outdoors learning, nor that play ultimately belongs to the children – not to the adults. However, a developmentally inappropriate classroom model disrupted early childhood for too many years. This wrong turn has required serious effort to re-establish an understanding of the importance of movement and to prevent the seriously negative consequences for young children who are expected to sit nicely and quietly.

Specialists like Sally Goddard Blythe (2004, 2008), organisations like Jabadao and the DVDs of Siren Films, with

LOOKING CLOSELY AT THREES

In Poplar Play, Chloe (2 years) carried a doll out into the garden. Anna (a practitioner) offered her a small-wheeled trolley for her doll. Chloe picked up a pillow, saw me looking and explained to me: "That's her pillow". Chloe spent time settling her doll into the buggy with the pillow. This action was not easy for Chloe, but she persevered. The problem was partly that Chloe was still holding onto the doll as she tried to get the pillow positioned to her satisfaction.

After several approaches to her problem, Chloe was satisfied with the arrangement and set off round the square of path in the garden. Chloe trundled the wheeled trolley around part of the path and showed Anna her doll. Anna looked carefully and admired, saying "you've got your dolly and her pillow".

At the same time Jerome (2 years) was working hard to manage a fair-sized trolley with a long handle. This was not an easy task for Jerome, who was quite small in relation to his chosen trolley. The square path in the centre garden had right angle corners and, in one corner, a wooden post supporting the veranda roof.

It took Jerome several goes to manoeuvre his trolley around this corner. But he persevered with a serious face of concentration – not at all unhappy. He used the trolley handle to work it a short distance back and forth until he got the trolley completely round the corner. Jerome headed along the straight and then worked a similar movement on the other corners of the square path, without the additional block of the post.

Jan White (2007) have made a significant difference to early years practice. These practical experts have explained and showed why physical development must never be treated as less important than other areas of children's learning. Specific physical skills matter for threes, and many examples are given in this section. However, the broad range of skills used in happy play support a broader and very important theme for physical development.

Young children need to become at ease in their own bodies and recognise what their limbs are doing. Lively, chosen play – not highly structured, adult-led activities – enables threes to continue to develop what has sometimes been called the sixth sense: that of proprioception or kinaesthetic feedback. Over early childhood, young boys and girls need to become more able to notice and interpret the messages of their own body.

Three-year-olds, who have enjoyed playful times as twos, toddlers and as babies, show a level of physical confidence that you can observe from the fact that they do not always have to check the position of their hands and feet. Their brain knows their body position for familiar activities. You will see threes looking carefully on less familiar physical activities, or when they are challenging themselves to try something difficult. Older children still do this check – as do adults in the same kind of situation.

Children, who live with a physical disability or chronic health condition, often need, and benefit from, an individually-tailored physical programme. However, in the usual course of events, threes do not need practitioners wielding a large file of planned physical activities, nor do they benefit from school-type PE. The significant contribution of Jabadao's approach to movement play (www.jabadao.org) has been to explain the importance of ordinary, playful activities and give early years practitioners the confidence to let young boys and girls relish their lively play. Children build their proprioceptive sense from clambering or running at different speeds, using a wheelbarrow to move materials, shifting wooden blocks with a friend. They need to feel, adjust and re-adjust the balance of their own body, along with any materials they are carrying.

An improving sense of balance for young children is also well supported by their keenness for rolling down a grassy bank, swinging to and fro and spinning. Threes, who have had time and space to hone their skills will manage more and more without adult help. However, they often enlist familiar adults for the more vigorous movements, or as

PARTNERSHIP WITH PARENTS: LIVELY THREES ARE NORMAL

Three-year-olds vary considerably in terms of physical skills and some will have more obvious confidence or co-ordination than others. You would be right to be concerned about any children with significant problems of balance and co-ordination in comparison with their peers. Undiagnosed problems with vision or hearing difficulties that affect balance might be an issue. Clearly you would talk with parents as well as make some careful observations of children, seeing whether some kinds of movement are harder than others.

Three-year-olds are naturally lively and, allowing for individual temperament, girls and boys need to move. They will become very restless and unhappy, if forced into sedentary activities. Sometimes you may need to address the unrealistic expectations of other adults: colleagues or parents.

Some children who live with ADHD may be noticeable at three yrs of age; because their significant struggles to attend and stay at all still are very different from their more normally active peers. Often you will give the reassurance that wanting to run and jump and shout is normal three-year-old behaviour – for little girls as well as little boys.

LOOKING CLOSELY AT THREES

In New River Green, four boys (mixed threes and fours) were very busy in the block area: a generous carpeted space with a large supply of wooden blocks, planks and shapes of different sizes. The boys were keenly building upright towers of the large open blocks. The aim was to build high, about as high as they could reach and then push the tower over, so that the blocks fell in a jumbled line across the carpet. The collapse of each tower was greeted with outbursts of delighted chortling. Each collapse was followed by a flurry of re-building, with the boys working well together in full co-operation.

A practitioner sitting with another small group at a nearby table kept an eye on the builders, but in no way cramped their style or the noise level, which was not excessive. On a couple of occasions, she gave a calm reminder that the boys check that there was nobody on the falling side of the blocks. There was space for this building and demolition activity and the practitioner let it flow. Two boys left and the remaining pair found 'Bob the Builder' hard hats and returned to a different style of building, which did not involve collapse.

tireless pushers on swinging equipment. Young children need plenty of adventurous physical play because it naturally stimulates their vestibular sense, also crucial to a sense of balance, imbalance and getting back in balance. Threes in lively play enjoy significant and sometimes quite sudden changes in position in relation to the surrounding physical environment. They temporarily escape the pull of gravity and then return to be grounded.

Of course, practitioners and parents need to take good care of young children, but this includes not being over-cautious. There is no need to stop games that threes clearly enjoy just because they stagger, temporarily off balance, or feel a bit dizzy and sit down giggling on the grass. By all means work alongside threes to build, or re-organise their obstacle course, but wait for them to ask for a helping hand. Offer, if you are uneasy, but trust a young girl or boy, if they indicate 'no, I'm fine'. Stop telling them not to climb that inviting tree and make sure they have a bed of leaves, or similar, for landing. If threes get stuck – in the tree or on the climbing frame – be close, but start by encouraging them to see how they could get down, rather than immediately lifting them to the ground.

Physical skills of three-year-olds

Individual three-year-olds vary in physical skills, confidence and awareness of the feedback of their own bodies. It is not unusual that they still bump into people or furniture, especially if they are absorbed in a task. Yet if three-year-olds are focused on an activity then they can be very detailed in their movements. Sometimes three-year-olds look 'clumsy' compared with older children. They can find it hard to change direction or stop, especially when moving at speed or to allow for other bodies close by them. Three-year-olds can handle simple games props. However, the careful looking and body co-ordination required for kicking a ball accurately over distance is beyond their ability. Yet, three-year-olds can be keen kickers and chosen practice is exactly how they improve their skills.

Threes can copy simple sequences of movement and often enjoy this kind of game in a small group, perhaps accompanied by music or song. Three-year-olds can have gained some of the finer movements of co-ordination,

LOOKING CLOSELY AT THREES

In Poplar Play there was a child-sized trampoline that offered a good springy quality, with a bar for children to hold as they bounced up and down. During my visit, I watched as children of different ages thoroughly enjoyed this piece of equipment. Their activity showed individual differences as well as the developmental progress of the skills needed to work the trampoline. Practitioners were present in the garden, should children have needed any assistance. But they trusted children to keep safe, even these boys and girls who were all 2-yr-olds, with the exception of Isobelle who was a rising two.

Jerome and Michael were on the trampoline together bouncing well. They called out "bouncy, bouncy" as they went up and down, and their practitioner accepted her role as the one to count their bounces.

Then Isobelle and Jack had a go. The difference between these two children was striking. Isobelle looked as if she was enjoying herself going up and down, but she was moved mainly by Jack's vigorous bouncing. Isobelle bent at the knees and tried to lift off. But for the time being, she had trouble co-ordinating for the bounce and both her feet stayed on the trampoline. Jack, about six months older, bent his knees and launched well for the bounce, with both his feet leaving the surface at the same time.

Later in the day, Jack was back on the trampoline with Tom. They both bounced with great confidence and controlled their movements from their legs as well as holding onto the bar. They avoided any crashes into each other. Jack showed that he could also manage an open-scissors movement of his legs within his jump before landing back on the material surface.

shown through their self care and helping out in the daily routines. Their enjoyment of art and craft activities also highlights their ability to direct and control movement. However, many threes are still learning to work tools like scissors; especially to cut paper or cloth – both of which have an irritating tendency to fold around the scissors. Threes need careful, unhurried practice with woodwork tools, but they can become safe in this year with hammers or saws. Also the looking and adjusting skills needed to do jigsaws is still hard for some three-year-olds; they will improve with practice and a bit of help.

The large movements are as important as the fine ones. Three-year-olds have a range of large physical skills: lifting, carrying, climbing, running and jumping. Rising threes and the younger three-year-olds may still be struggling with some co-ordinations, such as how do they launch off to jump with both feet at the time.

Three-year-olds have improved balance, although some are still wobbly. They may be able to stand on tip-toe, which is hard until they master the different balance involved. These young children can be confident in riding three-wheeled bikes and the three- and four-wheeled scooters that are now common. It is worth recognising that bike or scooter riding is a cluster of skills that take practice and concentration. Children have to work out how to get on and off bikes, how to make the pedals go in a steady forward action, how to steer and how to stop.

LOOKING CLOSELY AT THREES

An entertaining physical game in Poplar Play showed not only the physical skills of some children, but their awareness of their peers.

Chloe (2 years), Charlotte (3 years) and Kayleigh (5 years) were busy working the four-seater rocker. The rocker was on a spring and the girls were competent in making the equipment move in deep dives and back up again.

Two other children, Alric (3 years) and Jack (2yrs, 6mths) had tried, but found the vigorous rocking a bit strong for their taste. The girls had swiftly stopped the rocking to let each boy get off without complaining.

Kayleigh had the longest legs and used her body to steady the rocker on some occasions. As the youngest and smallest, Chloe slipped a bit from a firm seating once or twice and the other girls slowed to let her re-position herself.

LOOKING CLOSELY AT THREES

In Mary Paterson Rumpus Drop-in, Rebecca (3yrs, 3mths) created a substantial wooden railway layout. (See also page 17). She had created a closed loop of track which crossed a bridge. However, it was very difficult to move the train along the tight turn from the end of that circuit to cross the bridge and then on to the gentler loop that ended in buffers.

Rebecca persevered with the difficult task of how to get back to the bridge section and then round. She became frustrated, saying: "The train is broken" and "Mama, why's the train breaking?". Rebecca had tried to turn the train directly into the tight curve to the bridge. (Probably the only way would have been to reverse the train around the loop and back to the bridge.)

However, Rebecca did not give up; she tried different strategies. Finally, she chose partly to turn the train onto the bridge and partly to remake sections of her long train to be lined up on the next section. Then she announced: "We go again". The carriages and train were repositioned and able to go over the bridge, through the tunnel and round the top curve.

All this time Rebecca's mother was a friendly presence, but allowed her daughter to make the decision about how to solve this practical problem that mattered to her.

LOOKING CLOSELY AT THREES

In Poplar Play, Michael (2 years), Alric (3 years) and Charlotte (3 years) were all at a table with a special kind of jigsaw. The materials comprised a person in separate body parts that could be fitted together like a jigsaw. Then bits of material could be chosen and laid across to create clothes. A top flap was then brought down and the image created of a dressed person.

The group of four children focused on this activity. Charlotte did the actions but they all seemed to be contributing to the choosing of materials. They tried several different combinations of the small swatches of material to create different outfits for the jigsaw person.

Kayleigh, Marcella and Simone (all 5 years) enjoyed this activity slightly later in the afternoon. Watching them, it was noticeable that these older children were more able than the threes to line up the material straight across the completed figure. They were also able to smooth the material down so that the flap could shut more tightly. The enjoyment level looked very similar between the 3-yr-old small group and that of the 5-yr-olds, but the latter group showed more dexterity with their fine skills.

Three-year-olds playing with friends often use their physical skills in construction and pretend play games. These young children may struggle somewhat on joint activities. It is one thing to work out how you alone carry boxes or bricks in order to make a construction or help in tidying up large items. It is a different set of co-ordinations and communication skills to carry a large item with your friends and manoeuvre it into place.

When you observe threes, you will notice how much concentration they pour into chosen physical activities. They are ready and willing to try different ways to achieve their aim and confident individuals will have a good try before they ask for help. The very fact that they can ask for help – a given in early years provision with an encouraging atmosphere – seems to help young children to make efforts that are impressive from the perspective of their current skills.

Physical health and well-being

Many of the three-year-old physical skills are shown through their self-care. The usual tasks of dressing, eating and managing in the toilet are complex sequences of actions that young children need to learn through relaxed time to practise. Their growing sense of competence supports feelings of confidence and self worth and should never be underestimated within any early years framework.

The enhanced interest in physical development and activity over early childhood has been partially led by worries about sedentary childhoods and the impact on health. It is right to be concerned for young children who have already developed the habit of inactivity.

However, this concern must also focus on past, serious misjudgements in some early years practice which have promoted sit-down activities to the detriment of children's self-chosen play, especially outdoors. Since the majority of babies and young children are active out of choice and like to be on the move, it takes persistent adult discouragement to create little couch potatoes – in a nursery or the family home.

Enjoyable physical activity supports children's overall health. Active, physically busy children burn up their calories, work up a genuine appetite and enjoy their food. Physically active children are often then more able to rest fully, because they have been active during the daylight hours.

Physical activity helps children to build up strong muscles, suppleness in the joints and bone density.

The worst combination is when children, who have learned habits of inaction and a preference for passive activities, have also been allowed to learn unhealthy eating habits: constant snacking and a poor range of food. Such a lifestyle can lead to clinical obesity within childhood and makes children and adolescents vulnerable to health problems such as type 2 diabetes. This condition used always to be called 'late onset', because it was associated with a sedentary, unhealthy life style in middle age.

Healthy eating habits are about good quality food and drink, plus establishing a clear pattern of mealtimes. Young children need to experience what it is like to feel a bit hungry, to satisfy that hunger and to feel full, at which point you stop eating.

The serious disadvantage of letting children snack is that they do not build the habit that food is for satisfying hunger pangs. Snacking, especially as part of hours sitting in front of a screen, becomes just something that children do with their hands, another source of low level stimulation.

Relaxed, social mealtimes build healthy eating habits, led by familiar adults who eat good quality food with the children and take opportunities to set a good example for courtesy at the table.

Sometimes people talk as if you have to persuade children into eating good food, like fresh fruit. In most cases, you just have to put it in front of them when they are still young children.

In Poplar Play, I sat at the lunch table and dessert was a bowl for each table of orange and melon chunks, cut into the right size for little hands. These bowls all emptied with

PARTNERSHIP WITH PARENTS: SELF-CARE SKILLS

Best early years practice shows full respect for nurture and gives time for children to hone their skills for sharing in their own care routines. Your good example will encourage parents, if this is necessary, to value time for their daughters and sons to become more independent in three-year-old style. Young children deserve time for the pleasure of showing that now a task is 'easy peasey'. There should be no sense of a tick box approach: that a child can do up their buttons so that is the end of it.

They also deserve having an adult show appreciation, rather than any sense of at three-years-old, or any other age, the child 'should' be able to manage this skill. This approach is mean-spirited of grown-ups and is discouraging for children. Problems are more likely to arise when early years practitioners have been made to believe that 'care' and 'early education' are two separate areas, and that 'care' is the poor relation. Best early years practice will show to families that all young children need a nurturing, home-like atmosphere, wherever they spend their days.

LOOKING CLOSELY AT THREES

Active involvement in their own care and routines is an ideal way for 3-yr-olds to practise and apply skills.

During my visit to Burnwood Nursery School I could see how the children were active in nursery routines. The nursery had a self-registration system at the beginning of the day or session and a self-service drink and snack time.

Children had help whenever they wanted, but they were enabled to organise their own part in this relaxed routine.

During the morning, I was watching a 3-yr-old at the drinks table and inadvertently caught her eye. She looked at me and smiled, while unfortunately continuing to pour out her drink from the jug into her beaker. I noticed and at the expression on my face and words, she looked down and righted the jug. There was a spill on the table but the practitioner close by was calm and completely uncritical. She gave the child some paper towel sheets and the child mopped up the table without any distress. The approach was that of 'accidents happen sometimes' and this young girl was competent to right the situation.

no persuasion at all from the adults. The fruit was eaten with obvious relish at all the tables, along with spontaneous conversation amongst the three- and four-year-olds about what the different fruit was called.

I also attended a fruit-tasting day at a local drop-in run by Brighton and Hove Playlink. The children were young, many of them just rising twos, and there was great enthusiasm for all the different kinds of fruit that had been bought for tasting.

At the end I was sitting at a table with some of the mothers and one had a nearly two-year-old on her lap. The young boy was taking his time selecting fruit one piece at a time from the large bowl on the table. He looked carefully, moved in with a finger and thumb movement to pick a piece. Then he held it up and looked questioningly towards his mother. Each time she named the piece of fruit, he popped it in his mouth and then looked for his next bit.

Three-year-olds are likely to understand some aspects of bodies and health but it will be a very individual pattern, reflecting their experience. Three-year-olds are interested to learn about bodies and health but in ways that relate to what makes sense to them. Young children ask questions, share experiences and show their current knowledge with interested adults.

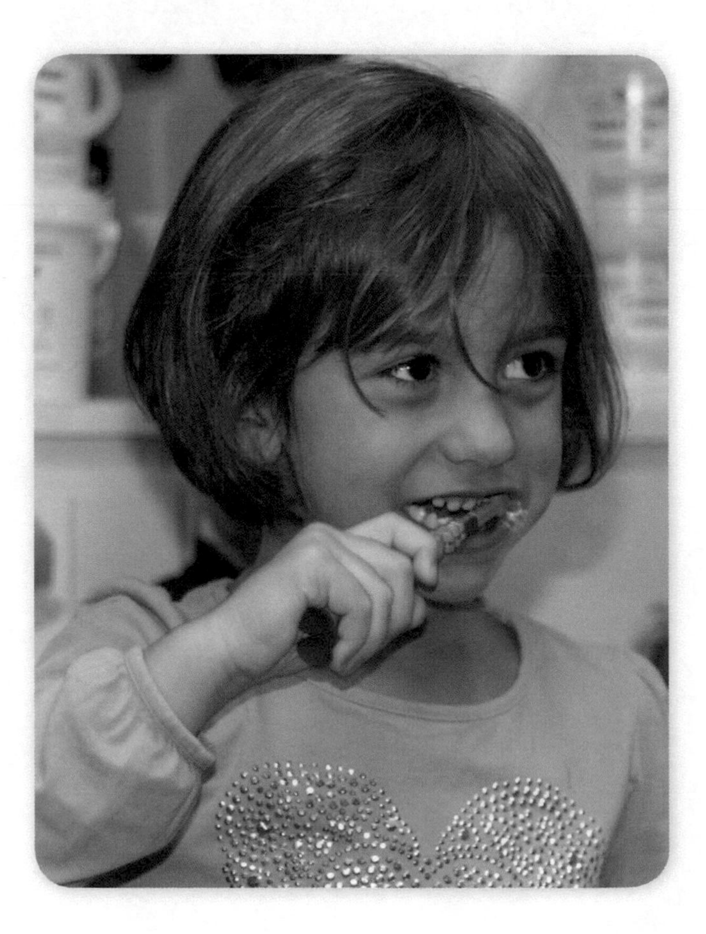

LOOKING CLOSELY AT THREES

At New River, Green Rosie (3 years) rubbed her head at one point and I asked: "Have you had a bang?". Rosie said confidently "no" and then informed me that "if the sun comes out you get a headache. If somebody bangs you, you get a headache".

Threes are closely interested in minor injury and consolation. In Poplar Play Centre, Michael (2 years) had slightly hurt his finger. He showed the finger to a practitioner who expressed sympathy: "Did you hurt your finger? How did you do that?". Chloe (2 years) and a second girl were close by and they moved in to see and listen.

Later, when we were sitting inside, Charlotte (3 years) showed me a scrape (very minor) on her leg. In response, Alric (3 years) pulled up his trouser leg to show me his scrape (almost invisible) as well. They wanted acknowledgement and interest from me, not massive amounts of attention. The examples are a reminder that for 3-yr-olds what happens to their own body, and that of their friends, is of great interest.

Literacy

The revised EYFS (2012) for England includes significant changes in the early learning goals (ELGs) for the end of the early childhood phase.

Regrettably, the minor changes to the literacy ELGs have continued to ignore the well-informed objections to developmentally unrealistic demands for five-year-old achievement in this area of learning. In the wide age-band of fives, some older children will reach the standards of the literacy ELGs.

However, many fives – notably the summer-born children – will still be at an earlier stage of 'proper' reading and writing and they are not developmentally delayed.

This issue is addressed in more detail in *What does it mean to be four?* (Practical Pre-School Books, 2012), but needs raising here as well.

Developmentally unrealistic expectations for fives will affect fours, and serious educational bullying will push into the year that children are three. It happened before with the misguided 'literacy hour' and, unfortunately, I still encounter 'letter of the week' for threes.

Oral communication is the foundation

English is an especially complex, non-regular language and our young children need more, not less time to make the challenging connections between the spoken and written language. The ELGs of the revised framework are still more applicable to most six-year-olds and this is the age at which their peers on the European mainland are usually expected to have cracked the written code of more regular languages.

Three year-olds are on the road towards literacy. Some of the older threes understand that writing exists, and recognise some familiar words or logos. They are building up valuable experiences through play, involvement in meaningful routines and getting out into their local neighbourhood. Like their four-year-old selves, the threes deserve a relaxed, not harassed, learning journey. They need to be fully supported in developing a positive disposition to learning about this reading and writing business. Literacy is not only about technical skills. Young children need experiences that build their personal conviction that reading and writing are useful skills for them and not something to be tolerated because the adults want it so much.

LOOKING CLOSELY AT THREES

At New River Green, there were sustained conversations at the play dough table. Vanya (the practitioner) remained sitting there and sensitively managed the beginnings and ends of the different conversations, depending on what the children wanted to tell her or inform the other children.

Sometimes the focus was the dough itself and children's plans. Yet often the conversation focused on completely different topics, as children arrived and wanted to chat, for instance about Winnie the Pooh and many details of Bob the Builder.

James (3 years) wanted to tell Vanya about last night. "I were snoring", he announced with a grin. James' ungrammatical phrase is very normal for threes. Vanya asked him "who told you that you were snoring?". James explained: "My Mummy. Sometimes I snore". James asked a question about when people snore. Vanya explained that "people only snore when they're asleep". James laughed and claimed: "My Mummy's snoring today". Vanya laughed in reply, saying: "Is she having a sleep?".

Best early years practice supports a three-year-old's learning journey towards literacy by continued support for the communication skills of talking and listening. This firm foundation is supported by encouraging children's love of books and storytelling, an enthusiasm for singing and playing around words, along with a thorough understanding of how meaningful mark making steadily turns into emergent writing.

It is counter productive in so many ways to rush young children on to the specific skills of reading and writing. Yet the short-circuiting of spoken communication worsens the situation. Confident spoken language is so very important because young children need great familiarity with the sounds that make up their language in order, in time, to ease the transfer to the written version. They need plenty of experience of hearing and using sounds and sound combinations, within the context of growing a large vocabulary through ordinary, not highly adult-led, talking and listening.

Children need to use spoken language, questions and listening to extend their general knowledge and to explore ideas through words. Later on, five- and six- year-olds do not only need to learn the technical skills of handwriting and the challenging maze that is English spelling. These older children need to have plenty of ideas of what they can write about. They need confident language skills to plan, talk about and reflect on the detail of what they want to write. The emphasis for threes continues to be on personal interaction and genuine conversation.

When they are ready to have a real go at writing, older children are often keen to write down their own stories. Their enthusiasm and growing competence is supported by experiences at an earlier age, when adults will have been the scribe, following children's instructions over what to write. Children's requests to you to 'write it for me' are not always about narratives. Many threes have the knowledge of their personal world to want their own version of notices, lists of what to do and step-by-step instructions.

Sue Palmer and Ros Bayley (2004) described the vital strands to build strong foundations for literacy throughout early childhood. They pointed to listening, talking, music and movement and story time as the most crucial building blocks to support later reading and writing. Ros Bayley greatly promoted the value of singing, a rhythmic approach to storytelling and helping young children to 'keep the beat'.

Such experiences are really enjoyable for young children; you only have to watch their faces to realise this fact. Yet this lively activity also sharpens young hearing to rhythm, alertness to the sound patterns of spoken language. Nursery rhymes and chants are a pleasurable way of alerting threes to the beginnings and ends of words, and to what rhymes and what does not. Singing songs and rhymes is at a different, more deliberate pace, than natural conversation, even if you slow the pace with younger children. It feels right to emphasise words or repeated phrases in song; it is part of the enjoyment. Alongside this experience, threes also benefit from adult encouragement, often simply being an amused spectator, to their enthusiasm for playing about with words – showing the level of oral confidence they have already achieved.

Enthusiasm for stories and books

Threes can be enthusiastic about storybooks and have personal favourites. However, they can be just as keen about information books, which tell them about sharks or spaceships. Even young threes can show a thorough understanding of how books work, from the beginning to the end, turning the pages and something of the difference between written words and pictures. With positive experiences so far, threes show detailed recall of familiar tales

LOOKING CLOSELY AT THREES

In New River Green Centre, Rosie (3 years) and Ben (4 years) played together for a long time. Looking back over this observation I was struck by how the children guided the sequence of their play by talking to each other. They were voicing out loud the steps of their joint project.

Ben and Rosie started by building a see-saw structure with blocks and a short plank. They sat on it but the see-saw motion was not very successful. Ben said: "But it won't go". Rosie replied: "I'll get a bigger one" and then "I'm going to make my own". She moved a slight distance to another part of the block and began to select pieces of wood.

Rosie and Ben worked close by each other in the block area, making their own personal constructions but chatting together and standing back to assess what they had done. They confidently called for the adults' attention whenever they wanted direct admiration of their constructions so far. And at one point they stopped work to chat with the adults about the very heavy rain that fell in the previous night. Both children returned smoothly to their constructions, switching attention between chatting, building, finding pieces of wood and chatting again.

By now, Rosie and Ben had both made complex, long constructions using a range of hollow blocks and planks. Rosie announced: "We can go under it", but looked dubious as she scanned the construction. The practitioner commented: "Do you think it is big enough to go under?". The children experimented a bit and it was clear that they could not fit under or through bits of their constructions. This discovery was not a disaster and their play shifted to accommodate it.

PARTNERSHIP WITH PARENTS: LITERACY AT HOME

Young children learn a great deal at home. The revised EYFS (2012) has stressed the important role for early years practitioners in encouraging a positive home learning environment.

However, there needs to equal recognition that many parents are very active with their own young children. A laudable focus on the need for supportive intervention in the lives of some under-fives must never create the wrong impression that most families are disengaged from their children.

Your good example, and sharing anecdotes about individual children, will help committed parents to understand the early parts of their children's journey toward 'proper' reading and writing. Well-intentioned parents can be made unduly anxious, and may underestimate the value of what they are already doing at home.

You may work to encourage some parents to talk more with their threes and share books. But many parents just need their efforts recognised; they are already supporting their children in appropriate ways.

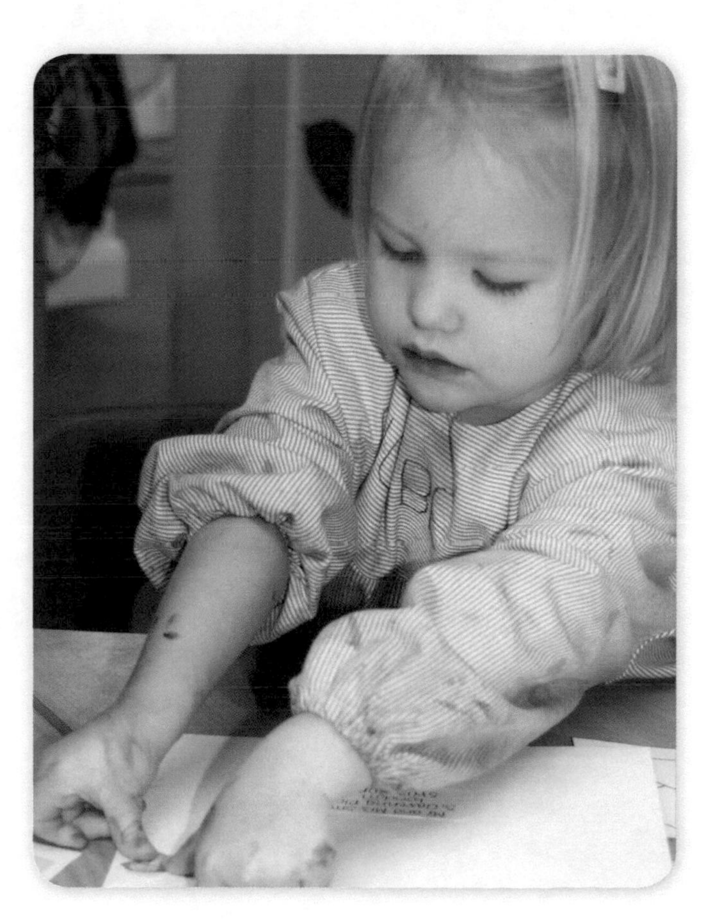

and are often helped by the repeating phrases that are an integral part to some books.

Some threes will be fortunate and stay with high quality early years provision – nursery or their childminder – for all their early childhood. The early years practitioners then have a thorough understanding of children's individual path towards literacy, or any area of learning. This situation applies even if in a nursery this understanding is passed with care from one key person to the next. However, many threes will have changed provision, or been a rising three when they joined a setting that does not take younger children. Their learning journey then started before you met these children. Given the unrealistic ELGs for literacy, it is important that a practitioner's knowledge rests on the whole story.

I would recommend Robin Campbell's (1999) account of 'Reading with Alice', his granddaughter, as a good example of the whole early childhood story. Alice, at three years of age, commented on and asked questions about many of her favourite books, although some she preferred to hear in silence. She liked repeat readings of books and had memorised parts of stories, joining in with whoever was reading to her. Alice recognised some words in her storybooks. She played at reading to herself, her toy animals and to her (real) baby sister. Alice liked stories but was also beginning to understand that there were different kinds of books. Robin Campbell gives the delightful example of how Alice (3yrs, 6mths) described a gazetteer of maps as: "It's a 'which way you're going' book". Alice's pattern is individual, but what aspects can you recognise of three-year-olds you know well?

Three-year-olds can really enjoy books but storytelling is also oral communication. Threes relish using simple props and supported by a guiding adult, learn a great deal from their active involvement in storytelling and storymaking (Stevens, 2012). Three-year-olds, who have been encouraged, can sometimes recount their own personal narrative: of what they have done with their family or you, and of interesting events.

Confident three-year-olds and rising threes will sometimes fill in the gap, when they do not know a word, with 'this and 'that' or expansive gestures. You help this story by being equally enthusiastic about 'do you remember when…' shared moments. These experiences are easily fuelled by happy experiences within your provision, but also by getting out and about in your local neighbourhood. You will plan the broad route, but there will always be unplanned events of interest. Young children will want to recount these to other children when they return to base, and often later through revisiting this interesting narrative with you.

Awareness of written language

Many three-year-olds are aware that language comes in a written form. Experience from family life as well as early years provision supports children to build this understanding bit by

LOOKING CLOSELY AT THREES

If young children join you at three years of age, your early conversations with their family will be to understand this child's current interests in terms of books.

Drew (my son) at just three years of age was very enthusiastic about books. He had enjoyed stories and looking at books since babyhood. He heard many books read to him by us. But from his toddler year he had independently accessed books as he wished from his own low shelf.

At 3-yrs-old he knew much of his 'Goldilocks' book by heart, some of the full-length Thomas the Tank Engine stories and parts of books he had heard in recent times. Drew liked to tell us the story of a book, turning the pages accurately as he moved along. He announced that he "was reading" to us. Drew showed clear signs of saying and practising newly bought books, so that he soon wanted to recount the story. For well over a year, Drew had showed a keen interest in information books and returned to his favourites again and again.

bit, with enthusiasm and a 'can do' outlook. Cathy Nut-brown (2005) drew attention to the useful concept of 'environmental print': all the writing, logos and other symbols to be seen in the local neighbourhood. The names of shops, of nearby roads and road signs provoke three-year-old interest and the growing understanding that these squiggles say something.

Logos and images also give a message, but young children need to realise that these are not writing. In a diverse area, young children also begin to understand that there are different languages written in the public arena, and some are in non-European scripts. Children will ask familiar adults: "What does that say?". Sometimes you will need to reply that you do not know, although you may be able to make a good guess from the context.

With a generous supply of paper, pens, paints and crayons, three-year-olds will have been drawing and painting for a long time. Threes have progressed in their meaningful mark making so that they choose to create curves, lines and different patterns in their chalking or large-scale painting. Some older threes are moving from creative mark making towards emergent writing. The pattern is very individual, but some threes start to distinguish their drawing from what they call 'my writing'. You start to see separate early symbols, some of which may be recognisable as close to letters. Much like threes' previous experience of books, you need to talk with newly-arrived parents in your provision, so that you ca make sense of this child's understanding of literacy, three-year-old style.

LOOKING CLOSELY AT THREES

In Mary Paterson Nursery School, Michael (a practitioner) and a small group of threes and fours explored stories using the magnetic board with bags of items for each story. They were retelling the story of Mr Grumpy and the car. The children were familiar enough with the story that they had fun at a couple of points by teasingly saying the wrong answer. At one point one child announced it was "Mr Bumpy", which got a laugh because everyone knew that was incorrect.

Individual children had magnetic backed cut-outs of the characters in the story. Michael checked with "who are you?" as he gave them out. A couple of children were confident enough to give a wrong answer deliberately and laughed, because they had clearly made a joke.

Michael read the story page by page and children placed items on the magnetic board as they featured in this part of the story. The children were held by a familiar story in which they could play an active part. They were also ready to recall which animal they were at the end of the story. They enjoyed echoing the familiar, repeating lines from the story narrative.

LOOKING CLOSELY AT THREES

In New River Green, Rosie (3 years) was in the middle of doing a jigsaw. She stopped and pointed, to direct my attention to a poster with different languages,. She spoke in a pretend language and told me: "I talking a different language". She smiled and did some more pretend non-English. She then returned to the jigsaw. There was absolutely no sense of making fun of any other language. Rosie showed her understanding that there were languages other than her own and that they sounded completely different.

LOOKING CLOSELY AT THREES

My daughter, Tanith, observed her older brother very closely. As a young 2-yr-old, she directly imitated Drew (then a young 4-yr-old) in asking us what specific written words said. At this age Tanith confused written letters with numbers and she thought all the marks 'said something'.

At just turned three years of age, Tanith wanted to have a go at writing her own name, just as Drew (then 5-yrs-old) was able to do with his own name. She recognised her name written down, but was still confused about the difference between letters and numbers. We wrote her name clearly and let her try in her own way.

At this point my daughter was known by her first name, which is Zoe. Over the year that she was three she had a go at writing her name when she wished, with no pressure from us. As a rising four, she was able to write Zoe clearly and liked to do this on her drawings. She had now worked out that letters were not the same as numbers. She knew numbers told you something different, although she was still working out quite what that was.

Close to her fourth birthday, my daughter told us she was fed up with being one of two Zoes in her nursery class. We reminded her that she had two personal names and some people chose not to use their first name. She said she wanted to be Tanith and was consistent in this wish. So we told her nursery and made the full switch. Tanith understood enough about writing to know that her middle name would look different on paper, as well as sounding different out loud. As a young four, she set about learning how to write Tanith rather than Zoe.

PARTNERSHIP WITH PARENTS: EMERGENT WRITING

In her presentations about emergent writing, Penny Tassoni highlights the importance of respect for children's mark making. As Penny explains, few adults would criticise a very young toddler for the early sound making of babbling and jargon. We would be shocked by someone who snapped, "don't be silly, talk properly!". Yet even well-intentioned adults are sometimes disrespectful about what Penny describes as the written 'babbling' of three- and four-year-olds.

Your good example needs to show to parents, when necessary, that young children's deliberate mark making is a vital step on the road towards 'proper' writing. If this mark making is called 'scribble', then the adult tone must be positive – maybe that it is 'scribble writing'.

Some threes have worked out that writing says something, often by observing how adults use their writing skills for a good reason. The young children want to have a try themselves, perhaps imitating older siblings as well as familiar adults. Some three-year-olds make pretend lists and want to write their name. All that is needed is a supportive environment, easy access to writing materials and respectful adult interest for what children tell you is their shopping list or a note for the milkman. Supportive adults follow children's interests; you are not pushing keen threes into premature writing. They are choosing their enterprise, and want your practical guidance.

Anne Hughes and Sue Ellis (1998) point to what should be a significant difference between early years provision and primary school. Early years practitioners should respond to young children when they choose to do meaningful mark making or emergent writing. Primary school teachers should still respond to children's interests and what they are motivated to write about. However, over-fives need to be taught to write, just as they need to be taught to read. This development does not just happen, especially with a difficult, non-regular language like English. So in primary school, teachers have to shift to recruiting children into writing following a shared agenda in the group.

The balance for best early years practice has to be much more on responding to the explorations that three-, and four-year-olds, want to make and the way they choose to apply their skills today. Helpful adults then support and extend the child's emerging understanding. Adults – practitioners or parents – risk seriously undermining children's motivation to become writers, if threes and fours are drilled by worksheet copying and tracing letters.

For threes (and fours too) the road towards becoming a writer is partly about what writing looks like and how you make letters with any accuracy. However, this process is equally about young children coming to believe the power of writing. Threes are already learning that writing is used for a whole range of purposes in real life: being able to write is so useful. As exciting as it is to talk directly with someone, writing lets you send them a message or leave one for later. Sometimes it is enough to voice your thoughts out loud, but writing lets you keep ideas for ever and tell other people about them, even when you have not met.

What are they learning?

Experts like Sally Goddard Blythe (2004) have identified the crucial links between respect for physical development and literacy. The large physical movements are just as important as the fine co-ordinations.

Three- and four-year-olds need to feel confident in their whole bodies and be able to respond to the physical messages of movement. Pressure towards early writing practice with young children is likely to cramp children's fine movements, as well as undermine the confidence of boys and girls who are not yet ready. In contrast, large movements build firm foundations for later handwriting skills, for instance, circling arm movements in playing with streamers and ribbons in a large indoor or outdoors.

Children gain hand and eye control and strengthen muscles through confident use of tools in painting, chalking, small-scale weaving, woodwork and other creative forms of purposeful play. Their hand and finger control steadily improves through shared enterprises such as using tools for gardening, pretend and real cooking and helping out with routines of tidying, wiping up and laying the tables with care. The skills for later handwriting do not exist in a little developmental bubble of their own.

A great deal of appropriate support for early literacy develops through meaningful use of writing in the learning environment. Threes also use meaningful mark making and then their emergent writing within their pretend play, when there is a clear purpose for using the skills.

There is currently a great deal of worry, and undue pressure, about getting young children to start reading and writing. We need to get the timing developmentally right and threes are too young. However, they are increasingly aware of writing all round them. It is important that the labels or notices they see are correctly spelled and punctuated.

A proportion of the early years workforce might not have been well helped by their own schooling. If you know your spelling needs attention, then do get yourself a pocket dictionary. It is positive for children to see you consider, and check, the spelling of what you write on notices or menus. Correct basic grammar and punctuation do matter; otherwise children see and start to absorb inaccuracies. Also, early years practitioners need to write up their observations and draft helpful reports for parents. Be honest – if your skills need some attention, and address the gap sooner rather than later.

WHAT ARE CHILDREN LEARNING?

In Buckingham's Nursery, (like other high quality settings I have visited) the children could see familiar adults writing for a purpose, such as recording what individual children had enjoyed for lunch. Adults often made observations in the room and children showed an interest in that activity. I was asked several times, courteously, by threes and fours what I was doing, as I wrote my own observational notes. Like the other adults, I gave a simple explanation that did not compromise the privacy of other children.

I observed one boy about to leave with his grandmother and he remembered that there was a note on the mail board by the internal door to the room. This practical idea was a board with each child's name and a fixed clothes peg, which could hold a note, letter for home or a drawing. This board was an innovation that made sense to young children, as this young boy showed. It was also a valuable message to children that writing skills were useful on a daily basis; in this case to recall and communicate something important between the adults.

LOOKING CLOSELY AT THREES

During my visits to Buckingham's Nursery, I watched threes and fours busy in their 'travel agency', using written materials available that related to choice of trips. One afternoon, children were especially keen to have their own sticky label written with their name and travel agency role on it. I noticed other examples when children spontaneously used writing materials within their play to a clear purpose.

On another visit, the children had organised themselves to take orders in their pretend café, having told me that I was to be the customer. They gave me a 'written' menu and were unimpressed when I expressed disappointment about the very limited range of sandwiches. I was told that I just had to choose from what was on the menu and they directed my attention again to the 'writing'.

Mathematics

Effective support for young children's mathematical understanding has to be based in a firm adult grasp of how the ideas develop for three-year-olds. As with other abstract ideas, practitioners and parents may be focused more on mathematical abstract ideas that make sense to them, rather than homing in on all the little steps along the way. Three-year-olds, within the meaningful context of play, regular routines and local trips, are busy learning a very great deal of maths. Familiar adults just need to spot that knowledge in action and recognise the blurry edge where young children are confused and want some help from you.

Practical maths

Three-year-olds are practical people; they grasp number, size, elements of shape and even something of the complicated idea of time within a familiar context. They want to build with blocks, transport stones around in the wheelbarrow, run their pretend market stall, have fair shares of apple crumble and know how long before they need to start tidying up. All of these purposeful enterprises need mathematical concepts – but applied in practice, not in the abstract.

Uncertain early years practitioners have sometimes turned to adult-initiated activities, thinking that young children will not learn without pre-planned mathematical events. Closer observation of child-initiated activities has often shown that a great deal of early maths is going on naturally through children's freely chosen play and conversation. Threes, especially the older threes are often counting out loud for their own purposes, using numbers in a practical way. Enthusiastic building and demolition uses a sense of space, spatial relationships, height and fitting shapes together or finding they will not fit. Best early years practice is to notice and work with children's self-chosen play and happy involvement in regular routines. You move on from three-year-olds' current understanding.

Children's skills are best improved with repeated opportunities to practise and threes are happy to 'do it again' when they feel they have a good reason. I have observed threes and fours have several goes, without prompting, to reach an accurate tally of items at snack time. Or they have wanted to count each other for a genuine wish to know 'how many of us are here today'. They use language for position and relative spatial relationships when playing with cars and roadways and building their railway tracks.

It is also valuable that threes see you using mathematical skills for understandable purposes. Just as young children need to see you reading and writing for a good reason, they benefit from seeing you count, estimate and measure with care. Young children happily copy us in shared enterprises; they do not need any persuasion to do so. Family life, and homely experiences within early years settings, are very appropriate for supporting children's early mathematical ideas. Children will explore some basic mathematical concepts in play, including their pretend play. However, the fuel for this enjoyable activity has to come from first-hand experiences, such as cooking with children and experiencing a real post office to make sense of their pretend one.

Numbers and counting

Threes are still in the process of understanding written numbers, and some children continue for a while to confuse the symbols for numbers with those for the letters of the alphabet. The written numbering system will only make sense to children who have fully understood what the words mean in practice. The main task for threes is often to grasp the idea of one-to-one correspondence: that you count by touching or finger pointing at each item in turn. Threes may be able to look and say for very low numbers: that there are two apples maybe. However, usually threes will have to count for accuracy. They are also likely to notice if somebody has taken something away; older babies and toddlers are alert to visible changes long before they can count.

Three-year-olds need plenty of practice getting familiar with number order: that you count up in the same pattern each time. Adults know that six follows five each time when you are counting higher numbers. However, we learned this fact a long time ago; it was not obvious at the outset. Three-year-olds are in the process of learning, and some have grasped the fact, that, if you want five bricks or three spades, you stop counting at that number, rather than go on and on until you run out of the numbers you know. Three-year-olds learn through watching peers or adults who demonstrate that it is useful to count by finger pointing or physically moving the bricks or spades to guide for when we have 'enough'.

Dorothy Caddell (1998) highlighted the great importance of thinking like a three-year-old, but with adult knowledge. Her approach was essentially that of tuning-in to a young child's world and considering 'what can numbers do for me?'. I know

LOOKING CLOSELY AT THREES

In New River Green Centre, Rosie (3 years) wanted me to look at the tank of tropical fish. She was interested to count the fish. First Rosie counted up to 8 and got confused. After a short gap she counted accurately up to 15, pointing to individual fish as she progressed. We agreed that the counting was hard, because the fish kept moving.

Later in the day, Rosie was sitting at the lunch table with a mix of other threes and fours. The children decided spontaneously to count how many children were sitting at this table. Rosie was an accurate counter, using her finger. Her one mistake was to forget to count herself – a common error at this age.

LOOKING CLOSELY AT THREES

Tanith at just 2-yrs-old recognised that written symbols said something, but did not have the understanding to distinguish between letters and numbers. She liked to say, "1, 2, 3, 4", but without reference to anything in particular. At two and half years Tanith could finger point to count a small number of objects. She liked to count up to 5 and sometimes made it to 10. At just over three years, Tanith could reliably finger point to count actual objects like books or bricks, up to 5-6 or more. She was confident counting up to 10, but liked some help with an adult voice joining in from 10 to 20.

PARTNERSHIP WITH PARENTS: POSITIVE ATTITUDES TO MATHS

In a similar way to the road to literacy, your good example needs to show parents how maths can make sense in the world of three-year-olds. In some cases you will confirm what families are already doing, however, for example, they may not have considered that active involvement of their child in food shopping was such excellent maths practice.

An additional issue with mathematics is that some adults – parents and practitioners – are profoundly uneasy about this area of learning because of their own unpleasant memories of school. Childhood emotions of confusion, the dread of making mistakes and feeling stupid can get in the way of being a helpful adult.

Some adults still seem to think it is alright to laugh and say: "I'm no good at maths", whereas few people would feel that being illiterate is amusing. Certainly, parents must not hear this message from early years practitioners. The key person needs to pick up sensitively from such a comment from parents. You might acknowledge that school maths was an unhappy experience for too many people. But then share and show what maths means here and now for the threes.

the reference is 'old', but I think it is still thoughtful for best early years practice. Young children learn through observing familiar adults, or sometimes through older children like siblings, using numbers for a real purpose. Threes do not learn this vital practical application from battery-operated toys or looking at numbers stuck at random onto plastic consoles.

Later on, the written numbers will make sense to young children as representing aspects of first-hand experiences. For instance, numbers are used for counting – useful to know: 'how many children are here for snack time, so how many cups do we need?'. But also numbers give us useful information, like 'how much money do we need to buy this book of stamps?' or 'how old is my brother?'. Numbers help us to make the right decision, for example: 'is this bus the one that will take us back home?' or 'what is the right oven temperature for cooking our carrot cake?'. Numbers can be used as part of playful activities, such as counting jumps on the trampoline, counting in hide-and-seek and in the many rhymes. Numbers can be used to impress, such as when children say they have 'hundreds and hundreds' of something.

Understanding concepts in action

Three-year-olds show that they understand a range of early mathematical ideas but the pattern is very individual. Helpful adults – at home and in early years provision – listen to what children say and watch what they do. You tune-in to what has caught children's attention and where their learning has taken them so far. The best adult planning to support early mathematical understanding is for experiences that integrate mathematical concepts in action. Young children need your adult planning skills. They cannot go on their own to shop for the ingredients to make scones, or head off to the local park to see the outdoor sculpture created from lots of cubes.

Once you have a clear perspective of what early mathematical thinking and action looks like, then you will spot the buzz of learning happening all around you. Within their play, threes talk in simple terms about size or shape. They comment on what they have done or plan ahead what they want to create. They look carefully and are able to see and judge broad similarities of amount, size or shape. They choose appropriately for their chosen task or use an effective try-it-and-see strategy to fit.

Three-year-old vocabulary extends to include their own words to compare and contrast: that something or someone is heavier or faster. Threes are aware of basic ideas of size and relative size of objects, although probably with the handy general terms of 'big' and 'little'. Through direct experience and use of their own chosen questions, young children begin to unravel some of the intriguing confusions. This pattern will be individual and helpful adults listen, watch and answer the questions that children want to ask. Some children wonder about 'bigness' and if something that is big will also be heavy, difficult to lift.

When you are an attentive play companion, you can make well-judged decisions, moment by moment, about adding

LOOKING CLOSELY AT THREES

One meaning of numbers for young children is that of age: a matter of importance when you are three or 4-yrs-old. Attentive adults who listen to 3-yr-olds' comments can gain a fascinating insight into young children's thinking and the ways in which numbers and other mathematical concepts begin to make sense to them.

Young children often relate numbers with age. A 3-yr-old in one nursery class looked seriously at me during a conversation we were having about birthdays. He said: "Did you know, you have to be three before you're allowed to be four?". I replied that I had never thought about birthdays that way before and that he was absolutely right.

Some children ask curious questions about the pattern of putting an age in the label of children's clothes but not in those sold for adults. It is a symbol of the confusing message to children that age in number is intermingled with size, as in 'when you're big, you'll go to school'. Of course, there is an age, rather than a body-size band, that determines primary school entry.

LOOKING CLOSELY AT THREES

In Poplar Play Centre, Alric (3 years) and Michael (2 years) were busy at the table with paper and 2-D shapes. The children could draw round the outside of any shape, but also inside to create an inner square, triangle and so on. Michael was keen but sometimes he drew inside the shape, rather like colouring in and sometimes he managed to hold a felt tip to the inside edge.

Alric had learned to hold the shape firm and could draw an inside line with confidence. He moved the triangle shape to make a whole series of drawn shapes on his paper, holding his felt tip in a fist grip. Alric looked very pleased and showed his paper to the practitioner: "Look at the triankles (how he said the word) I made them all!". The practitioner said the word triangle correctly, so Alric could hear but (rightly) did not ask him to repeat it. She focused on admiring Alric's careful work.

your comment. You can also make suggestions to young children who are temporarily frustrated, yet wait to see if they can solve the problem. When you are a friendly play companion, children will be confident to ask for your help if they need it.

At a basic level, threes are already using mathematical concepts to explore and solve problems in play, often in their construction, playing with trains and cars and other pretend play themes of their own choosing. They have some understanding of position and direction – again often shown through how they organise pretend transport or little play figures. Three-year-olds also make sense of abstract ideas through the medium of physical movement, the opportunities of outdoor play and of involvement in daily routines. Height, fit, 'too big for', 'too high for', 'just right' – all these ideas often become clearer because of playful experiences around climbing equipment, creative explorations with dough and from fitting play resources back into the right container or shelf space. Even fractions begin to make sense in an activity that children can touch and work upon in their own way.

Three-year-olds show complex pretend play, often with long sequences – some of which change without apparent reason, from the adult perspective. Threes test out baffling concepts like money in a pretend shop or café. This imaginary context works alongside real experiences of watching adults pay in shops, being able to hand over themselves and receive the change. Direct experience through hands-on activities is very important for young children. They cannot grapple with ideas unless they connect with what is in front of them at this moment.

There is no need to rush children onto precise language for size, shape or measurements and certainly not to restrict

LOOKING CLOSELY AT THREES

In New River Green, during a long run of sustained play with her close friend Ben (4 years), Rosie (3 years) announced that her structure was "a bridge" and put the plank, which was also her "water gun" back into place. But one of the uprights had shifted and she had trouble balancing the plank on the two uprights.

Rosie could see that her bridge was not level any more and said: "This is wrong". Ben's mother – sitting nearby – suggested maybe Rosie needed to move the upright. Rosie juggled the upright until it sat more firmly and then placed the plank on top once more. Ben's mother had waited to see if Rosie needed assistance, rather than moving immediately to help – a wise decision.

Rosie and Ben then together pulled clothes out of a basket that was available in the block area. They wanted to drape their constructions. Both children spontaneously named the colour of the cloth they were using and draped their own constructions with great care. Rosie was having more difficulty achieving the effect she wanted. Ben offered: "Rosie, do you want me to help you? You can help with mine". But Rosie replied: "I want to do it". Ben announced: "This is going to be lovely and blue and black".

After some more struggle, Rosie now said: "I can't put this on properly". Tessa (a practitioner sitting on a nearby table) offered: "Do you want some help?". She waited for Rosie's response and then moved closer as Rosie nodded. Tessa then asked: "How do you want it done?". Rosie explained: "All over the blocks". Tessa draped the cloth in the way indicated by Rosie's arm gestures and Rosie was happy with the result.

the adult view of mathematical learning to two-dimensional worksheets. Three-year-olds sometimes enjoy handling 2-D shapes but they also need the 3-D experiences. Three-year-olds do not learn about shape from a 'shape table'. In fact, such a focus does not make much sense until young children have visually tuned into the different kinds of shape. They have handled shapes for practical reasons and therefore have something definite to which they can link the shape word.

Three-year-olds do not understand clock time. It is not unusual that six- or seven- year-olds are still confused with telling the time. It is a complicated idea and children now face many different kinds of timepieces: analogue and digital. But time is much more than clocks and watches. In a reasonably predictable day and week three-year-olds understand about the sequence of what follows what: a practical and meaningful application of the concept of time.

Three-year-olds are learning how to manage their own time as they make choices about what they will do now and later. Rising threes and three-year-olds often have some idea of a few days of the week because something special happens on those days. Three-year-olds do not yet have a clear idea of the pattern of the named days. But perhaps 'Tuesday' has meaning because on that day this nursery always has a local trip or that 'Friday' is the day that this childminder and her children pay the milkman.

Abstract time measures like 'five minutes' or 'half an hour' do not mean anything to three-year-olds and not much more to four- or five-year-olds. Yet three-year-olds can make sense of: "We can look at one more market stall. Then we need to go back home for our lunch". Three-year-olds understand the passing of time and ways to indicate when 'time is up'. Nurseries often use a sand timer to support fair turn-taking on the bikes or other favourite equipment. Once they have become familiar with the system, it is not unusual to observe the timers being operated by children themselves – older three-year-olds and the fours.

Three-year-olds are often confused by timepieces, but this feeling emerges through curiosity and a willingness to ask adults to explain. I have listened to searching questions from three- and four-year-olds. They are often interested in what a clock or watch says. They are intrigued by different kinds of timepiece, for instance that a timepiece may be

LOOKING CLOSELY AT THREES

In New River Green, Jake (3 years) had flattened out his portion of red dough and was now carefully cutting into the dough with a pair of scissors. As he cut, he informed me that "this is a pancake cut in half and now it's going to be cut in half again". After some careful cutting Jake worked on merging the portions back into one pile, saying "I flatten it down, I want it to go on the other one".

LOOKING CLOSELY AT THREES

In New River Green, Jake (3 years) was playing with the Duplo® on his own. I sat nearby and he moved across to the train set. Jake talked out loud about what he was doing with the trains. His words were partly addressed to me but also seemed to work as self-talk to guide and plan his play.

Jake gathered up most of the carriages and the trains, saying: "I need all of these. Do you know why? Because I'm going to make two trains. And this one is going this way and that one is going this way". He indicated with his hand the different directions around the laid out track, which had a sloped section and several cross-over points.

Jake built the trains, adding carriages and took care to line up the magnetic dots that held the parts together to make a sequence. He showed understanding that the magnetism worked in one direction only. If the first fit did not operate to hold the carriages, then he confidently switched around so that it did work.

Jake took care guiding trains around the track. He had built trains with several carriages and getting them round the bends was not easy. There were crashes and trains tipping off the rails. Jake commented and explained to me as he played that "he's got to pull the one he banged" and "do you know how he's going to rescue him? If he does this like that" and demonstrated as he talked.

Jake explained how he put the trains together: "This will be the last carriage" and concentrated on fixing trains and carriages, lining them up on the track, moving them round and re-setting them as they tumbled off quite easily. In the end he commented about the scenario: "The trucks are very grumpy because they've been here a lot of years" and then that "the carriages have to hide in the dark tunnel because of the bumps" from the other train.

LOOKING CLOSELY AT THREES

One day, in Mary Paterson Nursery School, the children were welcome to make cloth bags, choosing the material and the shape that they wanted for their personal design. I watched as two 3-yr-old girls worked with the two practitioners who guided this activity. Teja supported children as they made their initial choices and Maryam worked the sewing machine, with children's active and safe involvement (see page 48).

On the table there was a wide choice of template shapes. When the child had selected the shape, then Teja helped the child to transfer the design onto paper with ruler. Their paper design had their name on. During the day, one girl wanted a circle shape and agreed with Teja that the best way to do it was to draw round a plate directly onto the material.

Individual children then chose from a wide range of materials for the main bag and also whether they wanted the same or different material for the bag handles. Teja then helped children to cut their material against the paper design. They would then confirm that the shape was right and needed no more adjustments. The 3-yr-olds whom I watched were excited to see their bag take shape and proud of the end result.

on the wall, on someone's wrist and even round their neck on a chain. As adults we know that these are all different kinds of equipment for telling the time, along with the digital display that is now commonplace on mobile phones and other handheld devices. Young children are in the process of discovering this information.

I sometimes use a stopwatch for observations. Some three- and four-year-olds look at it and want to know, "What's the time?". Some realise that the movements on the face are a bit odd and ask, "What have you got there?". It has been a challenging task to explain that my stopwatch tells me how long something has taken, rather than what time it is.

LOOKING CLOSELY AT THREES

One day, in Mary Paterson Nursery School, the plan was to cook vegetable soup in the afternoon. In the morning I accompanied Caroline (a practitioner) who was going food shopping with Sachin (3yrs, 9mths) and Beverley (4yrs, 3mths). It was late October and they definitely wanted a pumpkin, but their shopping list included other vegetables. A considerable amount happened on this relaxed outing, some of which was directly linked with the children's interest in practical mathematical ideas.

For example, at the main road, Sachin and Beverley spotted a fenced-off section with holes in the road. The two workmen saw all of us looking with interest. With the children by her side, Caroline asked the workmen what they were doing. They explained that they were replacing the water mains pipe. The children wanted to know about the depth of the hole, which was impressive, and the workmen gave them an estimate.

Caroline and the children took their time in choosing suitable vegetables and consulted their list for what they wanted and how many of each item. In the supermarket, Sachin and Beverley moved away a bit from Caroline in their search for items. They looked with care, picked and counted their carrots and onions. A double check with Caroline led to a decision that they had one too many cucumbers and they replaced one carefully on the shelf.

At the checkout, the children helped to load the items onto the conveyer belt and then placed them in their wheeled shopping trolley. Caroline managed it so Beverley could hand over a note and Sachin the coins. From his conversation, it was clear that Sachin came shopping with his family. On the way out of the supermarket, Sachin said: "My mummy lets me sit here". It was a row of chairs and Caroline suggested a sit-down with a slow count up to 10. They then set off back to the nursery, via a different route.

Understanding the world

Three-year-olds are interested and ready to be intrigued. Unless their confidence has already been dented, or their experiences very limited indeed, this age group are only too happy to explore, touch, feel, smell and generally find out about their immediate environment. A very great deal of finding out about their world requires that children have easy access to the outdoors and are taken out and about in their immediate neighbourhood (Lindon, 2012). Threes need thoughtful adults who start with ensuring that they understand the world through children's eyes, current interests and knowledge.

Extending children's knowledge

One of the great pleasures of spending time with young children is seeing and hearing their fresh outlook on the world at large. Your helpful support for extending threes' knowledge and understanding of their world must be geared to opportunities and a flexible adult approach to planning. Wise, developmentally appropriate practice, needs to be sensitive to these individual girls and boys now. However, threes cannot request experiences that they do not know are even possible. They cannot ask to go again to the woodland area in your local park until they have been at least once already.

Some first-hand experiences to extend children's understanding can happen within a very short space of time, maybe this afternoon or tomorrow. You can set off with a small group to buy material in the market or shop to resource the children's keen interest in capes for superheroes. Some events need to be planned a bit in advance, especially in group provision, although childminders often have to think ahead as well. You cannot just turn up at your nearest fire station and say 'we would like the tour'. Yet, with warning, this kind of service is usually only too pleased to welcome early years groups just as much as schools. In a similar way, a local dentist or nurse may be able to visit and chat with you and the children, but will need more notice than 'tomorrow'.

LOOKING CLOSELY AT THREES

The leaders and teams of Crescent I and Crescent II Kindergartens are committed to organising visits for their children – in walking distance and using public transport. I joined staff, parents and children (threes and fours) for their annual visit to Tooting fire station, London. The station has a strong community education programme and the team on shift that day was fully involved in a well-judged programme for the visit.

In their kindergarten the children had been able to play in recent weeks in a well-equipped pretend fire station. They had easy access to books about fire officers, engines and dealing with fires, but the children had also enjoyed these books in small-group times. They were ready to make sense of the real thing, and to take the experience back into their play.

At the beginning of our well-organised visit, we heard the emergency siren for the station, with the explanation that, if there was a real fire, the visit would need to end. But there was no emergency and we had the full experience. The children were able to clamber into a fire engine, a few at a time. They could touch the equipment on the engine and see everything up close, including one of the officers in full protective gear. We saw an officer hurtle down the pole more than once.

Everyone was able to have a go with the fire hose, adults as well, supported by a fire officer. It was possible to see the power of the water as he supported each child and adult to aim at a plastic chair set ready in the back outdoor area to the station. (It was wonderful!)

Threes, like any young children, need well-judged, adult-initiated experiences. Best early years practice has abandoned inflexible written plans that left minimal or no scope for the influence of children themselves – and that includes rolling, fixed topics. 'Next week' is not fixed because 'it's on the plan'. The only reason that Tuesday morning may be decided, for example, is because the local museum is expecting your visit. Other final decisions are made during this week, with a proper focus on short-term, fine-tuned planning, with the children.

Adult-initiated activities are open to extension, or shortening, because they are directly informed by the enthusiastic response from children. For example, it would be poor practice to change the post office role play area when the children are still busy doing post and running their office, just because the adult written plan was to move on at that particular point. There is no good reason whatsoever to close this local post office.

LOOKING CLOSELY AT THREES

Young children are often intrigued by the adult world, of work and generally what adults do, when they are not directly involved with the children. Readers who work in nurseries have probably had more than one conversation with a 3-yr-old who initially believed that you and your colleagues lived somewhere in the building.

It is well worth explaining aspects of the adult world and neighbourhood events to young children, although their full understanding often takes more than one conversation. During my visit to St Peter's Nursery Class morning there was a special event. The milkman who had delivered to the nursery for many years was on his last day and had been invited to join the end of morning group. The children were interested and some asked questions. Yet, their comments illustrated that these threes and fours were still rather perplexed about the milk, where it came from and quite what their milkman did other than arrive at their nursery. This event was not problematic; wise early years practice will never be to assume that children's understanding will become clear in one go.

Longer-term projects which extend young children's understanding of the world may be guided initially by adults' ideas, proposed for good reasons: that knowledge of individual children and this age group suggests strongly that they would be interested. Detailed projects also sometimes start with an experience shared by a young child. On a visit to Bridgwater Children's Centre I was shown a lovely 'Learning Story' book that was still in progress at the time. This narrative of exploration had started with one child coming in on a Monday morning thrilled to bits with having planted seeds at home over the weekend. The practitioner explained to me how other children listened with great interest and wanted to know "can we do that in nursery" and a child-initiated project was set in motion.

Delight in the natural world

There is always something to find and watch within an ordinary outdoor area. Practitioners do not need to set up these experiences; a garden area and time to explore will offer plenty of opportunities. Even small and apparently unpromising outdoor spaces will shelter little creatures and can be supplemented by plants.

The weather is always there for free and is a good focus for children's observation and speculation. They are interested in the current weather conditions and your practical conversations build on that basic knowledge. Looking outside, 'do we need Wellingtons?' or maybe you, as a responsible adult, say that it is 'definitely coat weather'. The different weather conditions are also a matter of looking ahead, of wondering whether it will rain while you are out in the park.

Threes are able, with a bit of support, to do some speculation: 'I wonder.../Do you think that…?'. Prediction of the weather, or any other natural phenomenon, is more than guesswork. Children need to draw on their current knowledge in order to consider what might happen. In terms of weather they need the practical conversation around 'how might we tell? What does the sky look like if it's going to rain soon?'.

If children are to extend their understanding, they need experiences and reactions from adults that support their curiosity rather than dampen it down. It is worth reflecting on your practice to check on who asks the questions: is it mainly the children? Threes express and satisfy their natural curiosity through comments and asking questions. They learn most by getting answers to the questions they want to ask today, right this moment. Adult questions can sometimes be useful, so long as they remain open-ended and speculative. The more closed the questions, the more a child is put on a 'do you know this?' spot.

Three-year-olds can be enthusiastic about the illustrations in books and information from appropriate television programmes or well-chosen DVDs. You may also find useful information on the Internet but, with threes, it will be useful that you do some searching first. However, threes need to explore a great deal in the real environment. Then they make connections between what they can see locally and what they find in books, or can only see in a DVD, because badgers come out at night or you do not get lions in the local park.

Children need the time to look and time to ponder. Sometimes they do not want to talk about what they are experiencing. Adults need to relax, look and listen as well. Now is not always the time to give information or ask questions. Children benefit from observing that you find this sight interesting or perplexing. Details matter to threes, but you have to listen in order to know what details are significant

LOOKING CLOSELY AT THREES

I spent an enjoyable day with 3- and 4-yr-olds in St Peter's Nursery Class. This team was very thoughtful about the experiences they provided for the children and the whole aim of their planning was to be able as adults to act flexibly within each day.

During the morning a small group of children found a really large spider in the outdoor sandpit. Adele (a practitioner) responded immediately to their excitement. She spent a long time bent over with the children watching the spider and chatting. Adele followed the children's lead and any questions from her were closely linked with what the children wanted to know or consider. It became clear that their main concern was how to keep this impressive spider safe so that the afternoon children could also see it.

The conversation flowed as Adele helped the children to consider possibilities. The agreed solution was to scoop the spider into a large jar, with a lid that had many air holes. The spider was viewed with great interest when the afternoon children arrived and then released back into the garden.

LOOKING CLOSELY AT THREES

At Buckingham's Nursery I observed an exciting, children-led event out in the garden. Some children found two snails and they brought them across to a little group in the upper garden. An adult made the simple suggestion that the snails could be put on the wooden lid of the large water tray. A group of children clustered round and were very excited and absorbed in the spontaneous snail race. Who might win?

They looked closely, talked animatedly about the snails, experimenting with poking a snail's head – gently – and watching as it retreated into the shell. Then, after a brief wait, it came back out again. The children stared closely at how one snail elongated its head and peered over the edge. With the adult's help, these 3- and 4-yr-olds later took the snails inside for closer study. Later in the day, the adult brought the snails back into the garden for the 2-yr-olds to see and the snails were released that afternoon.

Informal observation can easily track children's learning over time. For instance the 3- and 4-yr-olds in Buckingham's Nursery were persistently interested in snails and keen to find them. On other afternoon, several children gathered around the first child to spot a snail moving along the wood on the edge of the upper garden.

An adult and several children were again absorbed in enjoying this spontaneous event. The adult added words as appropriate about the snail, the shell and the fact that a child had also found one shell that was 'empty'. Later in the day one of these children asked me: "Where's our snail gone?" and I had to say: "I don't know". The child countered with: "He's gone under the ground".

On other occasions children were equally delighted and intrigued by spiders and a frog that most likely lived in a damp corner of the garden.

LOOKING CLOSELY AT THREES

I joined a group from Mary Paterson Nursery School on an afternoon outing that lasted two hours. The threes and fours walked to and from the park and were active the whole time. Each child had their own little bag, since the main aim of this autumn trip was to get conkers and also any leaves or other natural materials. However, a great deal happened on interest on the way (see page 44).

Once in the park, the children no longer had to hold hands, as on the pavement, and could meander. They did not dash, but covered the ground looking with care. There were not that many conkers and most were rather wrinkled and chomped. The children speculated with their familiar adults as to why this might be: perhaps this trip was a bit later than last autumn and maybe the squirrels had bitten chunks out of the remaking conkers.

The children collected plenty of leaves, the horse chestnut outer husks and bark. They, and the adults, had a fine time wading through the piles of dry leaves and kicking them up in the air. Everyone was also on the lookout for small branches and twigs to put in the kindling bag and take back to the fire pit located in the nursery garden. Children spotted several squirrels high up in a tree. They also had a good look at the bandstand area, which intrigued them. Children wanted to know what happened in this currently empty space and why there was a fence around it.

When we got back, the children had great enjoyment in showing the adults who had not come on the trip what they had gathered. They discussed the display in progress, which had some autumn leaves. They agreed that tomorrow they would sort out all the treasures and decide what to do. There was no rush.

to this individual child or small group. You may have taken the children to see the ducklings in the park, and these little creatures were indeed fascinating. But what the children want to talk about on the walk back is why some people throw their rubbish into the lake.

The local community – according to threes

Young children view the world from their personal perspective outwards into what they recognise as the broader social network for themselves and their family. Three-year-olds need a sense of themselves and their own community, before they can make much sense of the lives of people who live in a different community.

A nursery team who were based in part of a large building that included a leisure centre, once described to me how they had recently taken small groups of threes and fours for a walk around the centre. These children were entranced and keen to talk about the experience. They entered nursery through a side door and had no idea that all these interesting sights, many of which could be watched from the upper gallery of the centre, were part of the same building.

The nursery team was immediately responsive to the personal views of the children, recognised that the stroll had opened up new vistas for knowledge and understanding of the world of these young children. The team was definitely going to continue this internal visit on a regular basis.

The head and team of Mary Paterson Nursery School plan the day's staffing with care, with local trips in mind. They organise enough adults so that each practitioner has a child on each hand. I observed how the children chatted throughout the trip. This approach is far preferable to a walking crocodile with children holding onto a rope and handle system. Young children on a local trip need easy access to familiar adults and then three-year-old comments and questions flow easily. The leaders of Crescent I and II Kindergarten had made the same decision over how to walk locally. They planned ahead to keep the groups small enough for the experience to be personal for the children. For significant trips like the visit to fire station, forward planning ensured that enough parents or grandparents could join the trip.

Moving outwards from themselves

Three-year-olds, and under-fives in general, relate to their local neighbourhood. At this age, they need to spend time understanding and exploring what is close by: in walking distance or a short trip by public transport. Young children engage with their local neighbourhood by active involvement in choices related to visits out and about. An active approach to local trips supports children's personal and social development but also, of course, their knowledge and their understanding of a reasonably familiar world.

Best early practice is when practitioners engage closely in what intrigued the children. What do they want to revisit and what do they find interesting in a trip along the high road, to the market or local library? When young children have a clear idea of 'what my is neighbourhood like', then they can relate more to the whole idea that other neighbourhoods may look different in terms of people and the environment. Perhaps this photo of a street market looks different from 'my neighbourhood' and the children do not look exactly like 'me and my friends'. But they look as if they are enjoying buying fruit and vegetables 'just like us'.

Support for the development of positive attitudes has to build out from familiar experience for young children. It is unrealistic to aim to promote three-year-olds' understanding of a wide range of unfamiliar cultures or faiths, that they cannot experience in daily life that makes sense to them. Best early years practice is to look at what currently interests the children, what they understand and genuinely might comprehend, and build a little from that base. The connections might be to food or music, to family celebrations like welcoming a new baby, or to places and traditions that connect with the families whose children attend your setting. Young children cannot relate to a long list of celebrations or cultural traditions; they simply get confused.

LOOKING CLOSELY AT THREES

On the way to the park, with the group from Mary Paterson Nursery School to collect conkers, I could see that these threes and fours were busy looking and listening all along the walk to the park. They were able to get an adult's attention easily.

The children's points of interest included an excited "there's Luke's mummy". They highlighted passing the school attended by one child's big sister and spotting the house of a nursery child who was not in this small group. A blue balloon was swept across the courtyard by the wind, then a woman passed by with a handful of what the children and adults speculated were probably party balloons.

We stopped to have a good look at the outside of the underground station, for the children to confirm that this was definitely where the trains were. The children were also very interested in the flower shop and a barber's shop with its red and white candy striped pole. One boy explained where he had a recent hair cut and that place was called 'a salon' not a barber's shop.

Throughout the trip there were natural opportunities for road practice. We had to cross roads with and without a marked crossing. We had a black and white zebra crossing and more than one controlled by the red and green buttons. The children were watching other pedestrians as well as waiting for 'green man'. At one of these crossings, one 3-yr-old boy commented loudly and accurately that "he crossed on red man".

I was walking with a practitioner and two children in the rear of the group. We got a little behind the others, since Hari recognised the police station on the corner and wanted us to look at the building. Then he spotted a police car parked just up the road. We reached the police car and stood for a good stare. At that point, the two female police officers spontaneously offered for the children to get inside. The two scrambled into the front passenger seat and the police officer put the siren on – very exciting!

LOOKING CLOSELY AT THREES

In Crescent Kindergarten they create and explore a simple local map as part of getting to know children and families within the early weeks for a new group. The team make a modified local map that has space to show the location of the kindergarten and where children live. Most families live within walking distance, so it is possible to show everyone.

The completed map for each kindergarten group is fixed to the wall and available for consulting throughout the year. Children, with the help of practitioners and parents, can find themselves and their friends on the map and also the location of places they visit, like the local library.

Three-year-olds are focused on themselves as a natural part of their development. Their learning extends from their own perspective outwards in time and place. Three-year-olds begin to grasp something of personal history, through being interested in their own family and that of their friends. Three-year-olds are often intrigued – initially maybe disbelieving – that grown-ups, such as familiar early years practitioners, also had a childhood and have Mummies and Daddies.

A sense of place builds from three-year-olds' general knowledge of the local neighbourhood and journeys that make sense to them, because the trip has personal significance. Three-year-olds are interested in and keen to make sense of their local routes. They begin to build 'mental maps', like 'how we get to the library' and simple links between different locations. This development is much more effective when young children walk on a regular basis, rather than usually travelling as passengers in a car.

Three-year-olds have only a vague idea of distance. 'How far?' in measured miles is often confused for some years with how long it takes you to get there, which in turn depends on the mode of transport. But young children can gain an understanding and want to chat about 'my street/my shops/ my park', 'round the corner', 'a long walk away' or 'as far as Gran's house'.

Globes and maps do not make much sense yet to three-year-olds. They enjoy three-dimensional, small world play but symbolic nature of two-dimensional map representation is confusing and needs direct connections with children's first-hand experience.

Three-year-olds may begin to get an idea when the map concept links directly to their life. A local map can make sense when you use it with children as you walk a less familiar local route. They may see you consult train or bus routes if you take them on trips further away that need public transport.

Technology in daily life

The revised wording of the 2012 EYFS has usefully strengthened the message that children's learning about technology is not all about computers. Technology continues to be a broad term and the growing knowledge of three-year-olds needs to be focused on everyday technology: examples familiar to children from their home, early years provision and the local neighbourhood.

Three-year-olds are already interested in everyday technology and are able to use a range of domestic controls and appliances, some with careful adult help. Young children are usually intrigued by home technology, some of which will be replicated in their early years provision. Examples include remote controls, adults' mobile phones, the dials on the washing machine or a dishwasher and how to work the DVD player.

Apart from your commitment to extend young children's general knowledge, it is wise adult behaviour to teach children how to be safe around equipment that is part of their daily life. They will also be more able to accept that a small number of appliances are 'for adults only', so long as they feel trusted to handle and operate an increasing range of equipment that they can see matter in daily routines.

The revised EYFS (2012) has reduced the pages of welfare requirements. One useful change is the disappearance of the previous requirement on group provision to keep children out of the utility room or kitchen under all circumstances. All practitioners are, of course, required to maintain a safe environment and act so as to keep young children safe. However, the revised statutory framework now effectively trusts all practitioners to make wise choices about when children could, with an adult, be actively involved in loading up the washing machine or cooking in the kitchen during quieter periods of the day.

Three-year-olds are aware of high street technology such as the pedestrian crossing signals with the red and green figures, traffic lights and checkouts at supermarkets. They have often noticed automatic doors and the security CCTV screens that are so prominent in some shopping areas or train and bus stations. Children welcome local trips in which they have time to stop and stare. Some three-year-olds will start to integrate familiar technology into their play and their pretend play themes. They show an accurate grasp of how the real thing works.

There is no pressure to get any under-fives onto computers and certainly not threes. The toy industry has expanded into vigorous marketing of laptop technology and computer software – even for as young an age as babies – with claims that this toddler laptop or this DVD is educational, vital for young children's development. These claims do not stand up to scrutiny and far too many young children are spending hours in front of a screen, with serious consequences for their activity levels and general health.

Three-year-olds need plenty of experience with three-dimensional materials and hands-on activities. They need to value their own drawings and constructions and not risk the sense that they can never produce something as neatly and quickly as the software package. Some allegedly educational computer software directs children towards expecting quick reactions and reduces thinking time about what might be the correct answer as well as why this answer was incorrect. Some software is good quality, but you should always take a professional long hard look at any package. Consider – will this screen experience add anything to what threes could gain from getting their hands onto actual objects?

Expressive arts and design

Three-year-olds show evidence of imagination – that 'what if…' quality, the ability to pretend something is other than it is. They are also able to combine physical skills, memory and an experimental outlook to create different sensations and effects through sound and vision. When they are provided with a generous resource of basic materials, three-year-olds are keen to explore and happy often to share the results of that exploration.

The pleasure of creating something

With time, space and warm encouragement, three-year-olds show enthusiasm for making their own creations with arts and crafts materials. They make choices about the materials they want, simple techniques they wish to use, and when they would appreciate your help. A relaxed flow to the day allows threes time to think, but also to work on their chosen project, take a break – trusting that work in progress is kept safe, and return later in the day or on another day.

The example overleaf describes a shelf for work in progress. I have also known nurseries who, whenever possible, have enabled hard-working cardboard box builders or hole diggers to place a large 'work in progress' notice on their project. This kind of system shows respect for children and their enterprises. Additionally, when young children can work with a big store of recycled or natural materials, there is much less need for practitioners to negotiate turn taking or sharing out a limited resource.

Three-year-olds often want to explore variations around a theme. They may have become interested in swirls, a stripes effect or what happens if they fold paper. They apply their fine physical movements with careful and attentive looking as they use woodwork tools, build, work the play dough and create paintings and collages.

Young children also benefit from watching and listening to familiar adults who share interesting effects or demonstrate techniques.

Creative young children do not have to be left to their own devices all the time. Nor would it be best early years practice to leave them to struggle with tools without guidance. It is not adult interference to show and help, especially when asked. It is adult interference in creative endeavours to insist that children follow a given adult template, make it 'just like this' and tolerate adults' deciding when something is finished or is good enough.

As in other areas of their development, threes who are using their creative skills are also building attitudes about this kind of enterprise. When children's interest and curiosity is engaged, then they want to represent what they have seen and heard: through arts and crafts, imaginative play and recounting what was of interest to them. Over-directed three-year-olds will already show the signs of wanting to produce the picture that they believe an adult wants. Or they may sit and wait to be shown what they should stick and where in their collage. This passive outlook and self-doubt, may have developed from inappropriate adult standards from home, or unfortunately from attendance at poor quality early years provision. It will take time, but with encouragement you can build the confidence of these three-year-olds and get them back on a creative track.

A practitioner described to me, during a training day, a recent event in her nursery. A group of rising threes and three-year-olds had a grand time with glue and spreaders. They did not want to stick anything on paper that day. They were fascinated by how the glue could be swept and swished around on the table by a nifty wrist action with the

LOOKING CLOSELY AT THREES

At the woodwork table in New River Green, 3-yr-olds showed impressive powers of concentration, and they were allowed to take as much time as needed. These young children persevered with their saw, not an easy tool until you get the right technique. I watched several 3-yr-olds continue to work away, appreciating discreet adult guidance about the best way to saw, until they had sawn off their piece of work.

Some children chose to take their project straight to the adjoining table and make their choices about hammering in nails, or painting their wood. Other children took a breather, with their wood named and put safely on a shelf. Like other nurseries I have visited, the team at New River Green had created a dedicated shelf for children to place their work in progress. Children fetched their name card and propped it against their piece of word. All the children understood about this shelf. So, there was no chance that even a single piece of wood would be removed and used for another child's project

LOOKING CLOSELY AT THREES

On one of my visits to Mary Paterson Nursery School the children were welcome to make cloth bags (see also page 30). No more than two children were at the table working on a bag at any one time. But, because the activity was available for the whole day, any child who was interested was able to take a turn and no individual child was ever rushed with their project.

The children were able to use a range of tools and appropriate help was given by Teja for the cutting. However, the sewing was done on a proper sewing machine and a second practitioner, Maryam, sat at this part of the table.

Maryam guided the material through as the needle worked. But the children pressed the foot pedal to make the machine work. This was a joint effort with Maryam, who took care to say 'go' or 'stop', as appropriate. She showed children what they were doing at each stage of making the bag, such as how they were lining up the pieces.

Some children were especially interested to ask about the controls of sewing machine and Maryam explained the different working parts.

spreader. The children then explored spreading the glue on their fingers. The glue dried quickly and this group of young children had a highly focused time peeling the dried glue off one finger after another.

It was lovely to hear the practitioner describe this event with such respect for the threes. She and her colleagues had followed the children's wishes and placed the little piles of dried glue on display. They were ready to explain to parents why this material was so important to their children.

Art and sculpture

Threes who have been with you since a much younger age will have a background of happy foot printing, swirly creations with shaving foam or making absolutely anything from play dough. If children begin with you as a young three, then you will see the variety of past experiences in the group. Some three-year-olds and rising threes will head for your resources baskets and start making their collage with no prompting. Yet some three-year-olds may have next to no experience of open-ended creative activities that generate 'mess' that adults feel they have to clear up, with no help from the children.

Of course, three-year-olds should not be led to feel they are painting just for the adults to put something on the wall. However, children are often keen to have their artwork on display. The best approach is to work with the children about what will go on the wall, where and in what way. Supportive early years practitioners neither pre-organise nor tidy up the paintings or drawings of three-year-olds. If a child says that "this is my spaceship", then that description is important. They have not been directed to paint a pre-cut spaceship. Adults must not become focused on end products for their own needs. Yet there is nothing wrong with wanting something to show, so long as it is the children who want this. Threes, like fours, are sometimes keen to reach

LOOKING CLOSELY AT THREES

In Poplar Play, Charlotte (3 years) was working on some constructional materials at a nearby table. She used careful looking and feeling to line up her chosen pieces of wood. These items already had holes in them, ready to take a wooden nail or screw shape. Charlotte organised her materials and then hammered with care and concentration.

I was sitting nearby and she wanted to show me what she had done at each stage in her project. Finally Charlotte completed her structure to her own satisfaction. It had three wooden arms that rotated around the nail and she told me: "It's a clock".

LOOKING CLOSELY AT THREES

In New River Green, Rosie (3 years) showed her fine physical skills through what she chose to make, but her play also highlighted her persistent current interest.

In the first part of the morning, Rosie was at the dough table with three other children. She was working on her batch of dough and said to the practitioner: "It's a hiding place". The practitioner asked: "What's going to hide in it?" and Rosie said: "A baby's going to hide".

Later in the morning, when Rosie was doing a jigsaw with me, she extracted a carefully folded piece of paper from her pocket and said: "Close your eyes". She placed it in my outstretched hand. She had a small piece of paper coloured pink, with an even smaller piece fixed to the middle. Rosie explained: "It's a hiding place".

WHAT ARE CHILDREN LEARNING?

Burnwood Nursery School had a dedicated book corner but had made the decision also to place a range of information books around the nursery. So, children could consult arts and crafts books within the area resourced for drawing and other forms of creative expression. The children took good care of these books; they were not plastered with paint.

I saw a similar approach in Windham Nursery School where children could consult illustrated books about construction, located by the large block area.

Of course, children did not have to use one of these large books as they built. The point was that it was easy to look for a picture and chat about 'how to make a…' if they wished.

This informal distribution of books, which I have now seen in many nurseries, gives young children the clear positive message that books are useful sources of information and possible ideas, as well as where you find good stories.

Children are interested to explore different kinds of materials and, when you watch them, you realise how much open-ended creative enterprises also support children's physical skills and their concentration, when they are allowed to explore freely.

The satisfying end product for children can sometimes be surprising to watching adults.

that point when they judge their project is done. They want to show you and maybe their parents too at the end of the day.

Another aspect of creativity is a problem-solving experimental outlook. With familiar materials, three-year-olds will sometimes show a open mindedness to try different ways to make something work. Often three-year-olds need a hint or two from helpful adults, since they are still gathering enough experience to support a conceptual outlook that allows a situation could be other than what it is currently.

Three-year-olds can show technological creativity when they are given a rich resource of materials, many of which will be recycled. Young children especially relish the range of outdoor activities that raise practical 'how do we do it?' interesting problems. Access to space, time, natural materials and the chance to get seriously mucky are a real plus for many children.

Outdoor art and sculpture offer intriguing opportunities to young children. Some nurseries have the exciting possibility of time from an artist, but you will also find excellent ideas in articles in early years magazines. It often helps for adults to start with an idea and then threes and fours, especially those who have worked outdoors with you before, often generate ideas themselves.

A starting point may be a significant collection of twigs and branches, which you start by laying a simple pattern.

LOOKING CLOSELY AT THREES

As with almost any kind of activity in which children are engaged, a primarily creative activity will bring in other areas of learning for the child, as well as insights if you are watching and listening as an attentive adult.

In New River Green, Rosie (3 years) was keen to do a painting on the easel set up under the outdoor covered veranda. She beckoned me over to explain and show that she could not do a painting because the paper would not stay flat. Rosie pointed to the single bulldog clip in the centre and saying: "I can't do it". She demonstrated how the edges of the thick paper kept rolling inwards, as fast as she tried to flatten them. I suggested: "Do you think we need more clips?" Rosie looked closely at the easel and commented: "We need clips. We need one, two. We need two more". She pointed to the location as she said each counting word.

We went off together and asked a practitioner for clips. Fixing them was tricky for three-year-old fingers. So Rosie showed where each clip should be located, I hooked them over the easel and she pushed them well down. Then she took up her brush.

Very soon Ben (4 years) came to join Rosie. They painted peaceably together, each working with one half of the paper. Rosie looked at their joint painting and at Ben and said: "We're friends aren't we". The comment seemed to relate to the fact that they could share the same piece of paper and paint together. When their joint painting was complete, Rosie and Ben went off together to play with the small world farm that was in another part of the garden.

LOOKING CLOSELY AT THREES

In Poplar Play, Charlotte (3 years) and Kayleigh (5 years) were equally interested to sit at the table with flat trays filled with a pink thick cornflour mixture. Both girls were keen to explore the mixture and concentrating on using the available tools, including metal spoons and wooden spatulas.

Charlotte liked to feel and smooth the mixture with her fingers. Some of the mixture got onto her fingertips and she worked it off with care, finger by finger. She used the spoon to scrape and watch the mixture dribble thickly back on the tray. Kayleigh was more interested to use the spoon to scrape and carve patterns, then smoothing it out.

PARTNERSHIP WITH PARENTS: YOU CAN SING

Music is the area of creative expression in which early years practitioners and parents sometimes lack confidence. There is not usually the same level of unease as with maths, but some adults can feel 'my singing is so out of tune' or 'if only I could play a proper musical instrument'.

Of course, young children do not make these harsh judgements. They are happy that familiar adults sing to them from the earliest months of life. They like music and as toddlers soon join in any kind of music making – and they love dancing. At no point do they require that their familiar adults are public performance standard on any of these creative skills.

Adults who feel uneasy about singing sometimes feel better to sing along with a CD. There are many CDs of songs on the market. (One of my favourites is the lively approach of Steve Scott and Greg Bone: www.keepingthebeat.co.uk.)

Threes can also watch with interest as you experiment with a pattern in the earth made with some of the collection of pebbles. They will be soon busy with their own works. An outdoor sculpture involving wood may start with one or two items tied to an A-frame or a few ribbons tied to the fence. There is no reason for threes to inevitably discover outdoor art and sculpture for themselves, when many adults still think of painting as the indoor activity.

Three-year-olds are keen to look and to listen. They may already be able to express preferences about paintings that they like, just as they will have music they especially enjoy. Of course, creativity has to include choice for children. It would be poor practice for adults to insist that every child had to do a Van Gogh-type sunflower or are given a section that has to be painted blue in a large jointly produced mural. However, there is very good reason to extend the experience of threes and fours to different kinds of painting and individual artists.

Both Mary Paterson Nursery School and the Crescent Kindergartens took their young children to visit art galleries. These visits also involved the enjoyment of a longer trip on public transport. Both teams planned the visit with care: children were already familiar with the artist they went to see. The visit was focused on spotting a given artist or painting and the group took their time to have a good look. If the children had energy, there was a chance to look a bit more widely, but never to exhaust children by trying to do too much in one visit.

Singing, music and dance

Three-year-olds usually enjoy songs and singing. They show their powers of recognition and recall, not only in small group musical times, but also in the spontaneous singing that happy children start at any time. Children will vary a great deal, depending on their experience. If children join your provision as a rising three or young three-year-old, you will soon realise that some young boys and girls already know or recognise a range of songs and know the hand movements well. Some of their peers will have very limited experience and the chance to enjoy songs and nursery rhymes will be a fresh opportunity for them.

Three-year-olds are often very tuneful and this skill demonstrates their control of their language: the words, but also the varying volume of some songs, rhythm and emotional tone. They are also tuneful in their created songs and self-talk when playing. Three-year-olds sometimes play around with words, repeated phrases and tone. Some children already want to sing, dance or recount a story in front of a small familiar group and it is appropriate to provide the opportunity. However, some threes, as well as fours and fives, are not happy performers, or perhaps not of the kind of skill being required today. It would never be right for adults to insist; pushing a child into doing something in front of a group only encourages a strategy for more effective escape next time.

LOOKING CLOSELY AT THREES

In Poplar Play Chloe (2 years) and Charlotte (3 years) were sitting on either side of a wooden rocking seat. They worked it efficiently together by movements of their whole body and still managed to sing at the same time. First of all they sang several rounds of '1, 2, 3, 4, 5 – once I caught a fish alive' and then followed this song with an equally enthusiastic version of 'Row, row, row the boat'.

These two children had chosen to break into song and the observation is a good example of how threes, and younger children, will spontaneously starting singing songs or chants that they have learned with adults at another time.

Many young children enjoy the pleasure of dancing: the freedom of movement as well as choosing to follow the rhythm and pace of a particular piece of music. Three-year-olds often enjoy lively dance sessions, when adults join in as well.

Even young threes can move rhythmically and enjoy their own dancing as well as sometimes dancing with adults. Many nursery songs, rhymes and chants have associated movements, sometimes lively enough that the shared activity becomes a combination of singing and dancing.

Some young children already show an impressive sense of rhythm and are especially well able to follow a beat, even to keep in time with each other. In a nursery I used to visit in the east end of London, a small group of three- and four-year-old boys had drawn impressive looks during a shopping trip with a practitioner to the nearby market. Hearing the music from one of the stalls, the boys had spontaneously shifted into a rhythmic dance in tune with the music and each other, as they moved along the street.

I was struck as I looked through my observations for this book, and the others in the series, just how much we can view spontaneous singing as an unobtrusive measure of children's emotional security in their early years provision – nursery or childminder's home. Unhappy or uneasy children do not break into song as they work the rocker (page 23), nor do they make up tuneful little ditties as they do a jigsaw (page 12). Threes and fours, who feel under pressure, do not create spontaneous choral harmonies – a lovely event I observed in New River Green as a small group tidied up the home corner.

Imagination and pretend play

Three-year-olds demonstrate their creativity and awareness of everyday life through their pretend play. This exciting development is the visible evidence of threes' ability to represent what they have seen and heard through choices in their play. Young children take what they know of familiar life and routines and then play around with it. You will see the evidence of threes' observations and their thinking as they cook on their pretend stove or put the baby to bed. You support this important development with open-ended resources that young children can access and organise for their own purposes. Your other vital support is to ensure a range of first-hand experiences that children can choose, or not, to recycle back into their pretend play.

LOOKING CLOSELY AT THREES

In New River Green, the children gathered in a group after the end of lunch. For a short period of time it was quite a big group and the threes and fours were finding it hard to sit peaceably. A few children had wanted to hear a story and offered a choice of book. Sarah, the practitioner, judged the moment wisely and swiftly moved from the possibility of a story to some songs.

Sarah said, in a friendly way: "I think we're all too restless for a story. We'll have some songs". A child suggested 'Bob the Builder' and Sarah countered with: "We need to move. I think we need a song we can move to". She started 'Leo the Lion', a song with lots of movement, singing from loud to very quiet and then loud again. The children were delighted and wanted to "do it again!" and then a third time. They followed with several rounds of 'Head, shoulders, knees and toes'.

The children were happy and enthused. They had an enjoyable group time, with no nagging and now headed off for outdoors or other activities as they chose.

Many three-year-olds will also have enough experience from stories in books, television, DVDs and animation films to explore pure fantasy. When you listen and watch three-year-olds exercise their imagination, you are privileged to observe a window onto how they think the world works, what is important and what is interesting to these individual children.

There is of course a great deal of variety between children in what they want to funnel through their pretend play, but content three-year-olds will use their imagination in lively ways. Three-year-old fantasy play may be less complex than that of fours. However, with time and space they are well on their way to creating long-running pretend themes with each other.

WHAT ARE CHILDREN LEARNING?

In the nurseries where I made these observations, the practitioners had shared songs and rhymes with the children in enjoyable small-group sessions. But it was a credit to the positive social atmosphere, created by supportive adults, that the children viewed singing as part of life. The message from children's behaviour was that you broke into song when you felt content. It was another way of expressing yourself, and of course nobody would ask you to be quiet.

Best early years practice is to have the professional knowledge of how singing, music and musical rhythm is valuable for development of language, the road to literacy and is also supportive of deliberate use of physical skills. However, positive support for children over their early childhood will never be to view experiences mainly in terms of what they deliver for later. The main plot has to be that children have joy in their childhood; they only get one run at it.

Three-year-olds can be budding music makers, with simple musical instruments that enable them to keep time and rhythm. A few three-year-olds may manage to dance at the same time but this double co-ordination can be tricky. You need to make a variety of simple musical instruments and sound makers available for threes. However, it will probably not be sufficient to leave threes to get on with making music without any guidance.

Slightly older children, or experienced fours, may show the threes how to use the tools to create a pattern of sound with the saucepans on your outdoor music line. However, with physical skills like drumming it is useful for young children initially to play alongside an adult and see the different rhythms that can be created. You will not stifle young creativity by showing children what is possible.

Just as threes may already have views about pictures they like, they can also have opinions about their preferred music and request it. three-year-olds who have experienced a range of kinds of music can make choices as well as understand that perhaps a piece of music that 'sounds like the waves' is their music for the restful period after lunch.

LOOKING CLOSELY AT THREES

The regular local outings organised in Mary Paterson Nursery School are planned in response to observed interests of the children, but also on the basis of what is very likely to interest threes and fours.

I joined a walk to see two local building sites (see also page 16). The head explained to me that some children had recently been engaged in a great deal of building activity within the nursery garden. However, as she said, the opportunity to see two different sites in action was far too exciting to miss.

I was able to see the extensive building and digging that went on in the garden, including the large sand pit. Of course, like any interesting trip, all the children did not weave their experience of the building sites back into their pretend play. The success of an outing like this one is not judged exclusively by direct links into play. The interest and value for some children was seeing the real trucks and huge cranes. The pleasure was also in the opportunity to chat and notice all the interesting sights along the way.

LOOKING CLOSELY AT THREES

In the block area of New River Green Centre, Rosie (3 years) and Ben (4 years) played together for close to half an hour, moving seamlessly from one chosen focus to another, using blocks, wooden planks and stretches of cloth. At one point Ben decided that his structure was a rocket and then that it was an "astronaut". He sounded confused between the two and his mother (sitting nearby) explained simply that the astronaut was the person and the rocket was what they travelled in.

At another point in Rosie and Ben's long run of sustained play together, they both had pretend water guns in order to defend their block structure from marauding dragons. Later on, Rosie suggested that their wooden planks could be to shoot "very scary dinosaurs".

The practitioner sitting nearby and Ben's mother were consistent in letting the children's fantasy run unhindered, including Rosie and Ben's short excursions into pretend weaponry. The head and team at New River Green had discussed at length the question of superhero play and related weaponry. Like a number of other thoughtful early years teams, they had changed their practice from stopping this kind of play. They allowed the pretend play to evolve, unless there are genuine issues about roughness in play.

Further resources

EYFS (2012) Statutory and guidance materials

The Department for Education website is a good one-stop shop for EYFS materials. See: www.education.gov.uk/schools/teachingandlearning/curriculum/a0068102/early-years-foundation-stage-eyfs

This site provides access to:

- Department for Education (2012) 'Statutory Framework for the Early Years Foundation Stage: Setting the Standards for Learning, Development and Care for Children from Birth to Five' – this is the statutory guidance, including the safeguarding and welfare requirements, which applies to all early years provision up to and including reception class.
- Early Education (2012) 'Development Matters in the Early Years Foundation Stage (EYFS)' – the non-statutory guidance explaining the four main themes of the EYFS and providing some developmental steps along the way towards the early learning goals.

Books and websites

- Arnold C. (2003) *Observing Harry: Child Development and Learning 0-5*, Open University Press.
- Bilton Helen. (ed) (2005) *Learning Outdoors: Improving the Quality of Young Children's Play Outdoors*, David Fulton.
- Blythe S. G. (2004) *The Well Balanced Child: Movement and Early Learning*, Hawthorn Press.
- Blythe S. G. (2008) *What Babies and Children Really Need: how Mothers and Fathers Can Nurture Children's Growth for Health and Well Being*, Hawthorn Press.
- British Heart Foundation National Centre (2011) *UK Physical Activity Guidelines for Early Years (Walkers)* www.bhfactive.org.uk/homepage-resources-and-publications-item/280/index.html
- Campbell R. (1999) *Literacy from Home to School: Reading with Alice*, Trentham Books.
- Caddell D. (1998) *Numeracy Counts*, Scottish Consultative Council on the Curriculum.
- Chilvers D. (2006) *Young Children Talking: the Art of Conversation and Why Children Need to Chatter*, Early Education.
- Community Playthings (2005) *The value of block play*, (2008) *I made a unicorn Children come first*; (2010) *Enabling play: planning environments* www.communityplaythings.co.uk
- Cousins J. (2003) 'Listening to four-year-olds: how they can help us plan their education and care', National Children's Bureau.
- Department for Children, Education, Lifelong Learning and Skills (2008) 'Language, Literacy and Communication Skills: 3-7 Foundation Phase', Welsh Assembly Government http://www.swanseagfl.gov.uk/learn_agenda/wag_resources/langlitcome.pdf
- Dowling M. (2005) *Supporting young children's sustained shared thinking: an exploration*, Early Education.
- Early Education 'Learning Together' (www.early-education.org.uk).
- Evans B. (2002) *You Can't Come to my Birthday Party: Conflict Resolution with Young Children*, High/Scope Educational Research Foundation.
- Featherstone S. (ed) (2006) *L is for Sheep: getting ready for phonics*, Featherstone Education.
- Featherstone, S. (ed) (2008) *Again, Again: Understanding Schemas in Young Children*, A&C Black.
- Healy J. (2004) *Your Child's Growing Mind: brain development and learning from birth to adolescence*, Broadway.
- Holland P. (2003) *We don't play with guns here: war, weapon and superhero play in the early years*, Open University Press.
- Hughes A. and Ellis S. (1998) 'Writing it Right? Children Writing 3-8', Scottish Consultative Council.
- Jabadao, undated, *Developmental Movement Play* Jabadao: www.jabadao.org/?p=developmental.movement.play
- Jones M. and Belsten J. (2011) *Let's Get Talking: Exciting Ways to Help Children with Speech and Language Difficulties*, Lawrence Educational.
- Lewisham Early Years Advice and Resource Network (2002) *A Place to Learn: Developing a Stimulating Environment*, LEARN.

- Lindon J. (2009) *Parents as Partners: Positive Relationships in the Early Years*, Practical Pre-School Books.
- Lindon J. (2010) *The Key Person Approach*, Practical Pre-School Books.
- Lindon J. (2010) *Child-initiated Learning*, Practical Pre-School Books.
- Lindon J. (2011) *Supporting Children's Social Development*, Practical Pre-School Books.
- Lindon J. (2011) *Planning for Effective Early Learning*, Practical Pre-School Books.
- Lindon J. (2011) 'Too Safe for Their Own Good? Helping Children Learn about Risk and Life Skills', National Children's Bureau.
- Lindon J. (2012) *Planning for the Early Years: The local community*, Practical Pre-School Books.
- Lindon J. (2012) *Safeguarding and Child Protection 0-8 years*, Hodder Education.
- Lindon J. (2012) *Equality and Inclusion in Early Childhood*, Hodder Education.
- Lindon J. (2012) *Understanding Children's Behaviour: Play, Development and Learning*, Hodder Education.
- Moylett H. and Stewart N. (2012) *Understanding the Revised Early Years Foundation Stage*, Early Education.
- Nutbrown C.; Hannon P. and Morgan A. (2005) *Early literacy work with families: policy, practice and research*, Sage.
- Palmer S. and Bayley R. (2004) *Foundations of Literacy: A Balanced Approach to Language, Listening and Literacy Skills in the Early Years*, Network Educational Press.
- Sightlines Initiative *Rising Sun Woodland Pre-school Project* (www.sightlines-initiative.com).
- Siraj-Blatchford J. and Morgan A. (2009) *Using ICT in the Early Years*, Practical Pre-School Books.
- Siren Films *Firm Foundations for Early Literacy, Falling Out* and the *Outdoors* series of DVDs www.sirenfilms.co.uk
- Stevens J. (2012) *Planning for the Early Years: Storytelling and storymaking*, Practical Pre-School Books.
- White J. (2007) *Playing and Learning Outdoors – Making Provision for High Quality Experiences in the Outdoor Environment*, Routledge.

Acknowledgements

I have learned a very great deal over the years from time spent with children, practitioners, parents, early years advisors and college tutors.

I would especially like to thank the following settings for making me welcome in visits from which I gained ideas and the examples used in this book: Bridgwater Children's Centre (Somerset); Brighton and Hove Playlink; Buckingham's Nursery School (Leek); Burnwood Nursery School (Staffordshire); Crescent I and II Kindergartens (Tooting); Mary Paterson Nursery School and their Rumpus Drop-in (Queens Park); New River Green Early Years Centre and Family Project (Islington); Poplar Play Centre (Poplar); St Peter's Eaton Square CE Primary School Nursery Class (Pimlico); Windham Nursery School (Sheen).

I would also like to say how much I appreciate what I have learned from working with Early Excellence, Sightlines Initiative, Siren Films and the What Matters To Children team.

My thanks to Penny Tassoni, who has always been generous in sharing her ideas, and Jan Dubiel for his thoughtful approach to outcomes and creativity. Warm thanks also to the team at Tooting Fire Station (and Crescent Kindergarten) for enabling me finally to visit a fire station.

I have changed the names of any children and adults in examples observed in actual settings. Drew and Tanith are my own (now adult) son and daughter and they have given permission for me to quote from the informal diaries I kept of their first five years.

My thanks to the staff and parents of Crescent I and II Kindergartens, Mary Paterson Nursery School, Grove House Children's Centre and The Little Rainbow Nursery for giving us permission to use the photos in this book.